BBC BRAIN OF SPORT 2

With the coming of autumn, sports fans
throughout the country start planning
their training schedules. For BBC
Radio 2's *Brain of Sport* series starts
then, with competitors facing questions,
both general and specialist, on a variety
of sports.

Whether or not you actually wish to
participate (and the 1982 elimination
quiz, faced by all competitors, is included
here for those who do), everyone – young
and old – can impress his or her friends
with the knowledge gained from the
questions and answers inside.

About the author:

Chris Rhys was educated at Millfield and St Luke's College, Exeter, and went on to be a Physical Education teacher and lecturer with the Inner London Education Authority from 1965–74.

He changed to the quieter side of sport behind a desk from 1975 as a freelancer. His first job with the BBC was in the Sports Unit as researcher for *Brain of Sport* in 1975, and, like Peter Jones, he has yet to miss a programme. A contract member of the Sports Unit since 1975 as statistician/producer, he is co-author of THE GUINNESS BOOK OF RUGBY FACTS AND FEATS.

BBC BRAIN OF SPORT 2

**Questions and answers from the
Radio 2 quiz game**

Chris Rhys

Illustrated by Malcolm Bird

BBC/KNIGHT BOOKS

The records in this book have been checked
up to 31 March 1982.

© British Broadcasting Corporation 1982
Illustrations © British Broadcasting Corporation 1982

*First published 1982 by the British Broadcasting
Corporation/Knight Books*

British Library C.I.P.

Rhys, Chris
  Brain of sport.
  2
  1. Sports–Miscellanea
  I. Title
  796'.076   GV706.8

  ISBN 0 340 28655 5
  ISBN 0 563 20086 3 (BBC)

Printed and bound in Great Britain for the British
Broadcasting Corporation, 35 Marylebone High Street,
London W1M 4AA and Hodder and Stoughton
Paperbacks, a division of Hodder and Stoughton Ltd.,
Mill Road, Dunton Green, Sevenoaks, Kent (Editorial
Office: 47 Bedford Square, London, WC1 3DP) by
Cox & Wyman Ltd., Reading, Berks.
Photoset by Rowland Phototypesetting Ltd.,
Bury St Edmunds, Suffolk.

Contents

Introduction

The publication of Brain of Sport 2, from the popular Radio 2 series, coincides this year with a landmark for the programme. Towards the end of 1982 we shall broadcast the hundredth programme in the series. The first, broadcast in September 1975, took place at the Old Cryptians Rugby Club, Gloucester. Last year's competition was the most popular yet, with applications from over a thousand would-be competitors, indicating the enthusiasm for sports quizzes in clubs, pubs, schools, and homes throughout the country.

The questions in this book are based on the 1980 and 1981 programme and have been updated accordingly. The elimination quiz is, however, the one set for the 1982 series. Records, though, are made to be broken, and Lester Piggott, Seb Coe, Steve Ovett, Bjorn Borg, Liverpool Football Club and the like, are a researcher's nightmare, so bear with us if a couple of new standards are set! To replace the commentary clips and interviews used in the programme, we have included a number of pictorial questions with the ideas taken from the commentaries, and supplied by the Southport Sports Quiz League.

Brain of Sport owes an enormous debt to Peter Jones, Radio 2's leading Sports and Outside Broadcasts commentator. Peter has been quizmaster since the very first programme, and despite travelling on other duties from Buenos Aires to Bucharest to Brisbane, has chaired every programme. His expert and sympathetic handling of the quiz has encouraged many a nervous contestant. To the producers, Michael Tuke-Hasting (who devised the quiz), Patricia Ewing, Paul Garside, Richard Maddock, and now Caroline Elliot, go particular thanks for the hours of administration, editing and guidance.

The winners, who have combined sporting knowledge with speed of thought and ability to react under pressure, are:

1975   Patricia Arthur (Birkenhead)

1976   Paul Hewitt (High Wycombe)

1977   David Ball (Liverpool)

1978   Julian Pincher (Telford)

1979   Tony Shaw (Grimsby and St Helens)

1980   Arthur Palfreyman (Matlock)

1981   Derek Heys (Horwich, Bolton)

In 1977–8–9 Graham Edge (Reading) achieved the remarkable feat of being runner up for three successive years.

1   1982 Elimination Round

The invitation to take part in the radio programme is open to all. Entry forms can be found in the *Radio Times*, and announcements are made in Sportsdesk and Sports Report on Radio 2. Entrants are then asked to come to their nearest BBC regional centre where they sit a seventy-question, written quiz paper. There is a forty-five-minute time limit, and the quiz is held at the same date and time throughout the country, so it is as fair as can be devised.

The elimination quiz is based on a variety of sports, includes regional questions, some easy, some not so easy, and some downright difficult. But it's hoped that at least everyone manages twenty or more correct answers. From these results, the top twenty-four contestants and a number of reserves are asked to air their knowledge on the programme.

So, start here, and see how you rate with the experts. If you can answer fifty-five or more of these questions then you have a fine chance of taking part in future programmes.

1 Which is the only other team besides Liverpool to win the Football League Cup in successive years?

2 Who gained the Bronze Medal behind Ovett and Coe in the 800-Metres at the Moscow Olympics?

3 Who was the England baggage man for whom the tourists played a testimonial match at the end of the 1981–2 Indian tour as a mark of respect for his twenty-five years' service?

4 Against which country did Wales have their only success in the 1982 Five Nations Rugby Championship?

5 Where is the home of the Royal and Ancient?

6 Who was the losing finalist in the 1981 Wimbledon Ladies' Singles Final?

7 Which London Football League club officially applied to join the Rugby League for the 1982–3 season?

8 Which jockey rode two of the five classic winners in 1981?

9 Nash and Dixon won a Gold Medal for Britain at the 1964 Olympics – in which sport?

10 Which current British Boxing champion lives in Toronto?

11 Who was the 1981 BBC Pot Black champion?

12 Who was world 500cc Motor Cycling Champion in 1956, and from 1958 to 1960?

13 Who were the non-League nominees for possible election to the Football League at the League's AGM in 1982?

14 Who captains the Worcestershire cricket team in 1982 and also was in a team which had topped the Football League division three in 1981–2?

15 He won an Olympic Gold Medal in 1960 after training in a steamy bathroom for six months prior to his event. Who was he?

16 He played his last match at the 1982 Rugby Union County Championship Final. Who is he?

17 Which Wimbledon Champions of 1981 are aged thirty-nine and thirty-six?

18 In which year did Max Faulkner become Open Golf Champion?

19 Who is the Reigning World Darts Champion?

20 Where did the 1982 Commonwealth Games take place?

21 There are two race-courses in the British Isles beginning with the letter 'R'. Can you identify them?

22 Whom did Tony Sibson outpoint in an official World Title eliminator?

23 Who is the former Rugby Union International, who, to the end of March 1982, had scored in every Rugby League game in which he'd played?

24 Who won the opening Grand Prix of the 1982 Motor Racing season?

25 Arsenal were reputed recently to have made enquiries for a player – but at least £4,000,000 would have been needed for his signature. Who was he?

26 Whom did Daley Thompson succeed as Olympic Decathlon Champion?

27 In which country is the Currie Cup both the major domestic Rugby and Cricket trophy?

28 A 1982 World Boxing Champion has exactly the same name as another World Boxing Champion who held the title between 1959–1963. Who is he?

29 In which major sport will the 1982 World Championships take place in Ecuador?

30 Who is the reigning European Open Golf Champion?

31 Who were the captains of BBC TV's *A Question of Sport* in the 1982 spring series?

32 In which sport is Maureen Flowers one of the world's leading players?

33 Name the grey which won the 1961 Grand National.

34 Larry Holmes holds the World Boxing Council version of the World Heavyweight title – who holds the World Boxing Association version?

35 Who is the only British boxer to have won two Olympic Gold Medals?

36 Which former World Champion started the 1982 Grand Prix season as the other driver in the McLaren team with John Watson?

37 Which is the only division one football side not to have provided a player for England at the end of the 1981–2 season?

38 Who was the last Briton to win the Olympic 100-Metres title before Allan Wells – his life being depicted in the film *Chariots of Fire*.

39 And in the same film *Chariots of Fire* – who was the Scot who won the other Gold Medal at the 1924 Olympic Games?

40 Who captained the 1982 Five Nations Rugby Champions?

41 Who retained his World Men's Ice Skating title in 1982?

42 She won her second Wimbledon Singles title nine years after her first success. Who is she?

43 Who was the first swimmer to break fifteen minutes for 800-Metres?

44 Which Rugby League team play their home matches at Ninian Park?

45 Which horse won the 1981 Grand National?

46 He was World Boxing Champion from 1970–2 and lost his last fight in January 1982 against George Feeney. Who is he?

47 Who is the only player to go on a Lions Rugby tour as a player, then coach, then manager?

48 Three London teams have won the British League Speedway title since its merger in 1956. Can you identify two of them?

49 Which team has twice knocked out British holders from the European Cup?

50 Who is Britain's fastest female swimmer – the 100-Metres freestyle champion?

51 He scored 248 not out for Middlesex against the Worcestershire attack at Lords making the highest score of the 1981 English season. Who is he?

52 Who scored five goals in a First Division game against Southampton in the 1981–2 season?

53 Whom did Britain's Angela Mortimer beat in the final of the 1961 Ladies' Singles at Wimbledon?

54 Which golfer holds the World Record for the lowest
score for 72 holes? His score was 255.

55 Which basketball team won the English National championships in the five years from 1976–1980?

56 Who was the last jockey to ride two hundred winners in
a season?

57 To whom did Jim Watt lose his World Lightweight title?

58 What, in a sporting sense, are Denim Osella, Theodore
and Candy Toleman?

59 Which country won England's 1982 Football World
Cup group qualifying table?

60 He made his test debut for England in the sixth and final
test against Australia at the Oval in 1981, and was born
in Bulawayo in Zimbabwe (then Rhodesia). Who is he?

61 In the 1976 Olympics, who won a Gold Medal in the
Women's Overall combined exercises?

62 Who was the 1979 flat race champion jockey?

63 Which British boxer was the last to win an Olympic
Gold Medal?

64 Bruce Penhall is the current World Speedway champion – for which club did he ride when he won the title?

65 Which sports film won the Oscar for the best picture of
1976?

66 Who was the first Welshman to win the World Professional Snooker championship?

67 Where were the 1904 Olympics held?

68 Alphabetically, which is the first Football League team,
not including AFC Bournemouth?

69 Who was the victorious cox of the 1981 and 1982 Boat
Races?

70 Which former Minister for Sport was a Football League
referee?

2   General 1

1 Of which sporting body is David Oxley the General Secretary?

2 Which man won the World Superstars Series for 1978, 1979 and 1980?

3 Who is the coach of the National Rowing Eight of Great Britain?

4 In motor cycling, who was the first man to complete a 100 mph lap at the Isle of Man TT?

5 In 1974, who was the last Briton before Barry Sheene to win the Motor Cycling World 500cc Championship?

6 Which Briton won the 1980 Power-bike International, beating Randy Mamola into second place?

7 Who was the World 250cc and 350cc Motor Cycling Champion in both 1978 and 1979?

8 What is the name of the Scot who was World Side-car Champion for 1980?

9 The United States have won the Olympic Ice Hockey title twice – in 1980 at Lake Placid, and in 1960 at another American venue. Where was this?

10 Which Czechoslovakian girl won seven Individual Gold Medals in Gymnastics at the 1964 and 1968 Olympics?

11 Two Ski-jumping events are held at the Winter Olympics; the 90-Metre Jump is one: what is the other?

12 Which Gold Medallist from the 1968 Summer Olympics took part in the American Four-Man-Bob team at the 1980 Winter Olympics?

Goals

Five goals which are used in six different sports: ice hockey, soccer, lacrosse, polo, outdoor handball and hockey. Can you identify them?

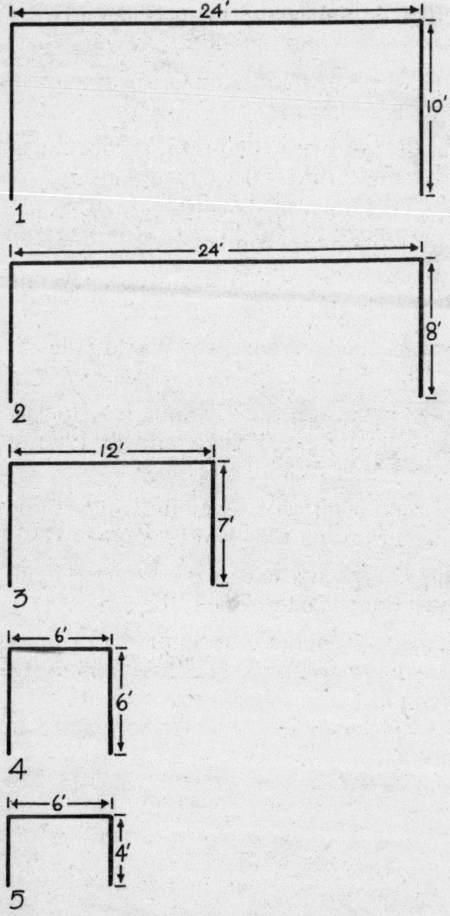

3 Soccer 1

1 With which non-League side did Malcolm Allison begin his managerial career?

2 Which non-League side knocked Liverpool out of the FA Cup in 1959?

3 Malcolm Allison has managed Crystal Palace twice, Manchester City twice, and Plymouth twice: which other contemporary manager has also managed three League clubs twice?

4 Who captained Brazil to victory in the 1970 World Cup Final against Italy?

5 Who was captain on the night that England drew 1–1 with Poland and so failed to make the 1974 World Cup Finals?

6 Which England player withdrew from the 1970 World Cup Finals for family reasons?

7 Before 1981–2, who was the last man, in 1970–1, to score 40 League goals in a season?

8 Before Leicester, in 1980–1, which was the last League club to achieve the Double over Liverpool?

9 Only three current First Division sides have not played in Europe. Two of them are Brighton and Notts County: which is the third?

10 Who has made the highest number of Football League appearances for Arsenal?

11 Whom did Tony Book succeed as manager of Manchester City?

12 Who was the last European footballer of the year not to play for a Bundesliga club?

4 Boxing 1

1 Before the Finnegan–Conteh era, who was the last Briton to be European Light-Heavyweight Champion?

2 Who was the last British European Lightweight Champion before Ken Buchanan?

3 Who was Britain's last European Flyweight Champion before Charlie Magri?

4 Who was the last British Heavyweight Champion, before Gordon Ferris, to lose his title in Round 1?

5 Which former World Champion competed in the 1981 New York Marathon, and in the same week was awarded his Olympic Silver Medal twenty-nine years late?

6 Who were the last brothers to win World Boxing titles?

7 Which boxer, with a son famous in another sport, was known as 'the Fighting Barber from Hanley'?

8 Who won the World Heavyweight title by beating Tommy Burns; and lost it to Jess Willard?

9 By what name was John Sholto-Douglas better known in the boxing world?

10 Which British Champion of 1981 fought Sugar Ray Leonard during the 1976 Olympic Games?

11 Who was the former World Heavyweight Boxing Champion whose sister had two Number One hits in Britain, and sang with 'The Supremes'.

12 John H. Stracey beat José Napoles to win the World Welterweight title in December 1975; which Briton *lost* to Napoles in a World title fight in 1972?

5   Athletics 1

1 Which woman was the only athlete to win two Individual Gold Medals at the 1981 World Cup in Rome?

2 Who ran his last race at Gateshead as a mark of respect to his greatest opponent?

3 Who were the 1981 Men's Inter-Counties Champions?

4 Who was the last Briton to hold the World 10,000-Metres record?

5 What is the name of the second Briton who ran a sub-four-minute-mile on 28 May 1955?

6 In which country did Sebastian Coe break the World 800-Metres record in 1981 – and gain his first World record of the year?

7 Which is the only field event *not* won by USA (men) at the Olympics since World War II?

8 There were two British husband and wife teams in the 1978 European Championships. The name of one pair was 'Wells': what was the other?

9 Who was the last athlete from a Communist country to hold the Men's World 10,000-Metres record?

10 Who was the 1981 Men's Inter-Counties Cross-Country Champion?

11 Up to the end of 1979, who was the last Briton before Sebastian Coe to hold the World Mile record?

12 Whom did Kip Keino beat into second place in the 1500-Metres at the 1968 Olympics?

Barrier Breakers

Who were the first seven British athletes to break the
four-minute-mile barrier?

6   Rugby League 1

1 Which player, between October 1977 and May 1979, scored a goal in each of 71 consecutive first class Rugby League matches?

2 Who, when he joined Hull Kingston Rovers in 1978, became Rugby League's first over-£25,000 transfer?

3 Which club did its manager, Eddie Waring, take to success in the League Championship, Challenge Cup and Yorkshire Cup, during the 1942–3 season?

4 Which was the last club, before Fulham, to join the Rugby League?

5 Which club, twice winners of the Challenge Cup, and founder members of the Northern Union, resigned from the Rugby League in the 1954–5 season?

6 Who was the first player to take part in both the John Player Rugby League Cup Final and the John Player Union Final?

7 Whom did Wigan beat in the first Challenge Cup Final to be staged at Wembley, in 1929?

8 Who, in the 1981 Challenge Cup Final, won his fourth winner's medal, whilst with his third different club?

9 Against which club did Wigan have their last Challenge Cup Final success?

10 Who were the winners when the last BBC Floodlight Competition was contested in 1979?

11 Who was Rugby League's first £50,000 transfer?

12 Who won the 1980–1 John Player Rugby League Final?

7   Soccer 2

1 Whom did Brian Clough succeed as manager of Nottingham Forest?

2 By whom were Liverpool defeated on their way to winning the Football League Cup in 1980–1?

3 Before 1982, three clubs have won the European Cup on one occasion only. Two of them are Manchester United and Celtic: what is the name of the other?

4 All three of Yugoslavia's 1978 International keepers are now in England. Katalinic and Borota are two of them: who is the third?

5 Which was Ron Saunders's first League management post?

6 Which was the last club to be promoted at the end of its first season in the Football League?

7 Which was Bobby Charlton's last game for England?

8 What is the name of the League footballer who returned to competitive football in 1980–1 at the age of thirty-nine?

9 Who resigned as manager of Carlisle United in the 1979–80 season, so as to take up a similar position with Hearts?

10 Which Third Division footballer left Britain to become leading scorer in the Dutch League with Ajax, and was also top scorer for Bruges before returning to the south of England?

11 Which club has remained for the longest period in Division I without winning the League Championship?

12 Which was the first Football League club to register all white as its first choice strip.

Expensive transfers

Who were the first ten one-million-pound footballers in
Britain?

8   Cricket 1

1 Who was the last Englishman to take ten wickets in an innings in First-Class cricket?

2 Which Pakistani has scored the highest number of First-Class runs?

3 Which man, with 989, took the greatest number of First-Class wickets in the 1970s?

4 Who scored the fastest century ever in the Gillette Cup?

5 Dennis Amiss scored 100 for England against New Zealand in a Prudential one-day match in 1973. The game was not played at a Test Centre: where did it take place?

6 Who is the oldest man to have played Test cricket?

7 Who, with a total of 34,380, scored more runs in his career than any other player who did *not* play in a Test match?

8 Which cricketer before Joel Garner in 1981, had the best bowling figures (4 for 10) in a Benson and Hedges Cup Final?

9 In the 1977 Centenary Test, who scored a century for Australia?

10 The very first Test match at Trent Bridge saw W. G. Grace play his last match for England; it also saw another famous player make his Test debut – the first of his 58 appearances for England. What was his name?

11 Who was the first bowler to bowl 20,000 balls in Test cricket?

12 Who was the Man of the Match in the 1981 Gillette Cup Final?

9   Speedway

1 Who won the 1980 Speedway National League?

2 Which British League team had three finalists in the 1980 World Speedway Final?

3 Who was the first American to win the World Speedway Title?

4 Who was runner-up to Michael Lee in the 1980 World Speedway Final?

5 John Louis and Kenny Carter finished second and third in the 1981 British Speedway Championship at Coventry. What is the name of the club for which they were both riding?

6 England International Dave Jessup joined the British League side King's Lynn in February 1979 for a record £20,000 fee. For which British League team did he ride previously?

7 For which British League side did Ole Olsen ride before he joined Coventry and led them to two successive British Speedway League Titles?

8 Which current England Speedway International made his debut in England's 67–41 victory over Australia at Swindon in July 1979 and then became England's youngest-ever International?

9 Who was the 1980 British League Riders' Champion?

10 Who won the 1980 Speedway Embassy Internationale?

11 Which country won the 1981 World Pairs Speedway title in Poland?

12 Which club went from the bottom to the top of the League and eventually won the 1980 British Speedway League?

10 General 2

1 Who held the World Record of 62 World Cup Skiing victories before Ingemar Stenmark in 1981?

2 Who were the 1981 holders of the 'Superbowl' in US Football?

3 In a sporting context, what have Lowestoft, Weston, Ramsgate and Weymouth in common?

4 Who are the reigning National Men's Basketball Champions?

5 Name two current Olympic events in which women compete against men as Individuals.

6 With which sport would you associate Karl Schnabl of Austria?

7 Who was the last Briton, before Gillian Gilks, to win the Singles title at the All-England Badminton Championships?

8 To whom did World Champion Geoff Hunt lose in an early round of the 1981 World Masters Squash title at Wembley?

9 Who won the first Men's Singles in 1977 in Badminton's inaugural World Championships?

10 Of which sport was Eugene Codrington of Great Britain the European Heavyweight Champion in 1978?

11 In which city did the 1980 RAC Rally start and finish?

12 Which woman won the English Open Squash title consecutively from 1961–76?

Baseball

These seven baseball teams have all been winners in the World Series. Can you identify their home towns?

11   Athletics 2

1 Sebastian Coe broke the World mile record twice in August 1981. Who finished second to him on both occasions?

2 Who was the last man to win the 100-Metres and 200-Metres titles at the same Olympic Games?

3 Who was the last American to win the Men's High Jump at the Olympic Games?

4 Who is the only male athlete to have won six Commonwealth Games Gold Medals?

5 Who was the 1981 Women's Inter-Counties Cross-Country Champion?

6 Who was Geoff Capes' coach?

7 Who was the last English male athlete to win the World Individual Cross-Country Championship?

8 On which track did Steve Ovett break his own World 1500-Metres record?

9 Who is the only female athlete to have won four European Games titles?

10 In which family, in the 1970s, were there three British record-holders?

11 Which man has won the *Emsley Carr Mile* in the fastest time?

12 Who is the only British female athlete to have won the World Individual Cross-Country Championship?

12   Golf 1

1 The British Open has been held five times at Royal Birkdale: which man has won the Championship twice at this venue?

2 On which course did Greg Norman win the 1981 Dunlop Masters?

3 Which former British Open winner was fined £70 in 1979 for attempted murder?

4 Who shot rounds of 63 – 66 – 62 – 64 in the 1981 Nigerian Open?

5 Who won the Centenary British Open in 1960?

6 Who holed in one in the 1973 British Open – fifty years after his first appearance in the Open?

7 Which course was used as a British Open venue for the first time in 1977?

8 Who, in 1974 and 1975, was the last man to win the Dunlop Masters in successive years?

9 Name the show business personality who lends his name to the Los Angeles Open.

10 The Bing Crosby Open is held on three courses – Spyglass Hill, Pebble Beach and . . .?

11 Who are the only father and son to have represented Britain in the Ryder Cup?

12 Who won the first British Open after World War II?

13   Horse Racing 1

1 Which is the only horse to have won the Ascot Gold Cup three years in a row?

2 Who owned the 1978 Derby winner Shirley Heights?

3 Which is Edward Hide's only Derby winner?

4 In 1980, on which course did Jonjo O'Neill break his leg when Sinbad was brought down?

5 Major Dick Hern trained Dunfermline, winner of the 1977 Oaks, for HM the Queen; which of the Queen's horses did he train to victory in the 1974 1000-Guineas?

6 What is the name of the last horse trained at Newmarket, before Shergar, to win the Derby?

7 Which horse has won the *Prix de L'Arc de Triomphe* in the fastest time?

8 Which year was the only Grand National in which Red Rum won as favourite?

9 Who was the only woman jockey in the 1981 Grand National?

10 Jim Wilson, in 1981, was the first amateur jockey to win the Cheltenham Gold Cup since . . . what year?

11 Freddie Head has ridden four *Prix de L'Arc de Triomphe* winners: which horse gave him his last success?

12 1923 was the last time when the Flat-race Jockey's title was shared: name either of the jockeys.

Race-courses

Can you identify the race-courses shown on the map?

14   Cycling

1 Which Briton was the World Professional Pursuit Champion in both 1972 and 1973?

2 Which British girl cyclist won a Bronze Medal in the 1980 World Road Race Championship?

3 In the 1981 Tour of the Mediterranean, which British cyclist beat Bernard Hinault, previous winner of the Tour de France three times?

4 Eddy Merckx shares the Tour de France record of having won eight stages on a single tour with another Belgian cyclist, who achieved the feat in 1976. What is his name?

5 Who was the last Belgian to win the Tour de France?

6 Which girl who had won a 1980 Olympic medal in another sport, also won a World Cycling Title in the same year?

7 Bernard Hinault of France won the 1978 and 1979 Tour de France. A fellow countryman had won the race in 1977: what is his name?

8 Who was the last Briton, in 1976, to win the Tour of Britain Milk Race?

9 In 1979, which Swiss rider won the World Professional Cycle Cross title for the fourth successive year?

10 In the 1981 Tour de France, the course went through three other countries in addition to France. Two of them were Belgium and Switzerland: what was the third?

11 Who is the only cyclist to have won the BBC Sports Personality of the Year Award?

12 Who, with thirty-four wins, has gained the highest number of stages of the Tour de France?

15   Soccer 3

1 Which was the first Second Division club to win the FA Cup?

2 Who, in July 1979, became the first Second Division player to be transferred for £750,000?

3 Which player scored in all three Gold Cup matches in 1981?

4 Liverpool beat Bayern Munich to reach the 1981 European Cup Final; whom did Real Madrid defeat in their Semi-final?

5 Two players, both born in Liverpool, made their debuts for the Full England International team against Brazil at Wembley in 1981. One was Peter Withe: who was the other?

6 Which club has won the highest number of post-war FA Cup Ties, up to the end of the 1980–1 season?

7 Which Football League club has suffered the greatest number of defeats at the hands of non-League clubs in the FA Cup since 1925–6?

8 Which is the only team to have played in the Scottish Premier Division, First Division and Second Division, since the formation of the three Divisions in 1975–6?

9 Name either of the clubs which in the 1980–1 season set a record for all FA Competitions. Seven matches took place before a winner was found for the FA Trophy.

10 Who was the manager of the Greek club Panathinaikos in the 1971 European Cup Final?

11 The highest score for the FA Cup Final at Wembley is 4–1, registered by two clubs. Derby County achieved this in 1946: what is the name of the other club?

12 In 1969, who played his hundredth and final game for Brazil against England?

16 Cricket 2

1 Who was the first cricketer to score 400 runs in an innings in First-Class cricket?

2 Who was the first cricketer to score centuries against all the other countries in a Test match before 1982?

3 Who was the last cricketer to score a double century in the University match?

4 Which County has been dismissed for the lowest score (23) in the John Player League?

5 In the 1975 Prudential World Cup, an Australian took 6 for 14 against England: what is his name?

6 Bob Taylor, when playing against India in 1979–80, became only the second wicket-keeper to take seven catches in a Test innings. Who was the first?

7 Who was the last South African to score a century in Test cricket?

8 In South Africa's penultimate Test match, which bowler took his 123rd Test wicket with his last ball in Test cricket?

9 Who, in the 1920s, made the highest number of runs ever made in a decade – 29,601?

10 Between 1968 and 1971, England played 26 matches without defeat: who was the only man to play in all 26 matches?

11 Which city lost a full day's Test play owing to rain in December 1980 – for the first time ever?

12 In the Benson and Hedges fifth wicket partnership, name either of the players who hold the record of 134 runs.

County Cricket

Who were the nine original members of the County Cricket Championship instituted in 1873?

17   Tennis 1

1 Who, in 1973, were the first winners of the World Doubles Championships?

2 The 1974 Davis Cup was won by South Africa, by virtue of the fact that their opponents refused to play them in the Final – on political grounds. Who were their opponents?

3 Who won the first Men's Singles Final at Wimbledon played between two left-handers?

4 Before the start of the 1981 Wimbeldon Championships, Bjorn Borg had won thirty-five consecutive games at Wimbledon. Who was the first person whom he defeated at the beginning of that remarkable run?

5 Who, in 1965, were the first brother and sister both ranked in the Top Ten in the USA in the same year?

6 Who were the runners-up in the 1981 Braniff World Doubles?

7 In 1981 a Brazilian made his 115th Davis Cup appearance in a career stretching back to 1962: what is his name?

8 Who beat Ann Jones on her first appearance in the Ladies' Singles Final at Wimbledon?

9 Who partnered Ann Jones to victory in the Mixed Doubles at the 1969 Wimbledon Championships?

10 In 1973, who was the last woman to win three legs of the Grand Slam? (Wimbledon was the only one she did *not* win.)

11 Who is the Wimbledon Referee?

12 Who was Ilie Nastase's partner when he won his first Wimbledon title – the Mixed Doubles in 1970?

18   Rugby Union 1

1 Who has made the greatest number of appearances in Tests for the British Lions Rugby XV?

2 Who holds the Individual British Lions Rugby record for the highest number of points in a Test match?

3 Which was the last provincial team to beat the British Lions?

4 During the 1977 British Lions Tour to New Zealand, three of the players on the tour were uncapped, and all three were Welsh. Elgan Rees was one: name either of the other two.

5 Before 1982, which was the only non-London side to have won the Middlesex Sevens since 1972?

6 There were only two Scots three-quarters on the victorious 1971 British Lions Tour to New Zealand. One was Chris Rea: who was the other?

7 Which is the only club to have lost two successive John Player Cup Finals?

8 Which scrum-half made a record twenty-four appearances for England between 1956 and 1962?

9 Who was the last Scot to be Tour Captain of the British Lions?

10 Two of the 1971 British Lions backs later joined Rugby League. John Bevan was one: who was the other?

11 Which rugby player set a record for this university by winning his fifth Blue in the 1980 University match?

12 Which first class Welsh team plays in All Black?

1 In which event in women's athletics at the Moscow Olympics did the same country gain first, second and third places – the first time such a result had occurred?

2 What is traditionally the first event of the Decathlon?

3 Which athlete was fourth in the 1981 London Marathon and was also the UK record holder for the 1500-Metres prior to Steve Ovett?

4 Two American cities have staged the Summer Olympic Games. One is Los Angeles: what is the other?

5 Since the time for the World Mile record went under four minutes, there has been only one instance of an athlete breaking the previous world record without actually winning the race. What is his name?

6 Who, in 1975, was the last Briton to win the World Cross-Country title?

7 Which race is often referred to as 'The Fell Runners' Grand National'?

8 Which British athlete broke a British record three times in one hour in a 1980 event – yet still lost to another Briton?

9 Steve Ovett has taken world records from Sebastian Coe; from which other Briton has he taken a world record?

10 Who, in 1967, was the only British woman ever to win an event in the Final of the Women's European Cup?

11 Who won the 1980 New York Marathon?

12 Who is the runner who just missed gaining an Olympic medal when he finished fourth in the 1500-Metres at the 1976 Montreal Olympics?

1 In which sport is Kevin Jolly one of Great Britain's leading players?

2 In which sport was Prince Philip a World Champion in 1980?

3 In April 1981, which club won the Women's Club Hockey Final?

4 Whom did Steve Davis beat 9–3 in the 1981 Final of the English Professional Snooker Championship?

5 In which sport, in 1976, did the United States beat Scotland to win the *Air Canada* Silver Broom World Championship in Minnesota?

6 With which sport would you associate 'Hairy Dog', 'Cut Lips', 'Twilight Beauty' and 'Spencer Bay Special'?

7 Which inaugural World Cup was staged at Port Erin in the Isle of Man in 1981?

8 Who was the 1981 British Amateur Rackets Champion?

9 Who succeeded Robin Cousins as European Figure Skating Champion?

10 In which sport is Jeremy Rogers of Lymington a British captain?

11 Who won the 1980 World Amateur Snooker title?

12 Who, in Crown Green Bowls, is the only man since 1955 to have won the Waterloo Cup twice?

Sports pitches

Can you identify the sports you would play on these pitches?

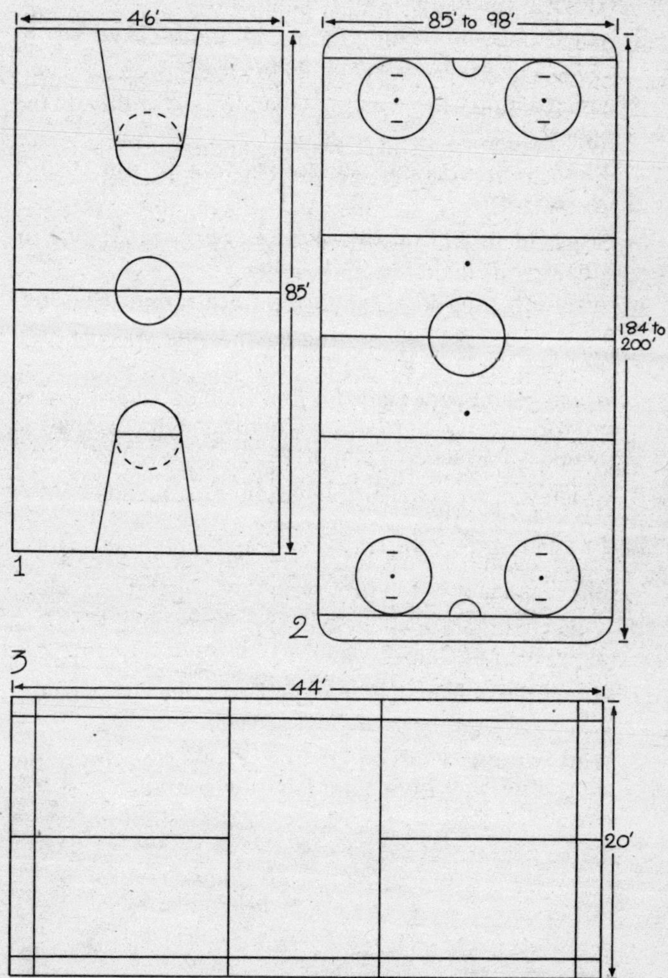

1 The last red cards were shown at Brisbane Road on 17 January 1981, where the first was also shown in 1976. Who was the first unfortunate victim?

2 Which club, by beating Orient 14–0, holds the record for the biggest away win in the FA Cup?

3 Which country has won the Olympic Soccer title on the highest number of occasions?

4 Which club knocked Sunderland out of the 1980–1 League Cup?

5 Which team started the 1981–2 season in August by scoring their first goal since January?

6 Despite having lost 2–1 in the third round, Charlton Athletic still managed to reach the 1946 FA Cup Final. Who beat them in the third round?

7 Which goalkeeper made his first team debut last season and within forty-eight seconds of the match – a Division 1 game – had saved a penalty?

8 Which was the last Third Division side to reach the FA Cup Semi-Finals?

9 Brian Clough lasted forty-four days at Leeds; which other manager lasted forty-four days, also at Leeds?

10 Which team did Jock Stein manage immediately before taking over at Celtic?

11 Who is the only man to have had his name taken in both 1981 FA Cup Final matches?

12 Who, with 46 goals, holds the record for scoring the highest number of Second Division goals in a post-war season?

We've Won the Cup!

Can you identify these soccer trophies, then name the *first* winner of each and the team which has won them most often?

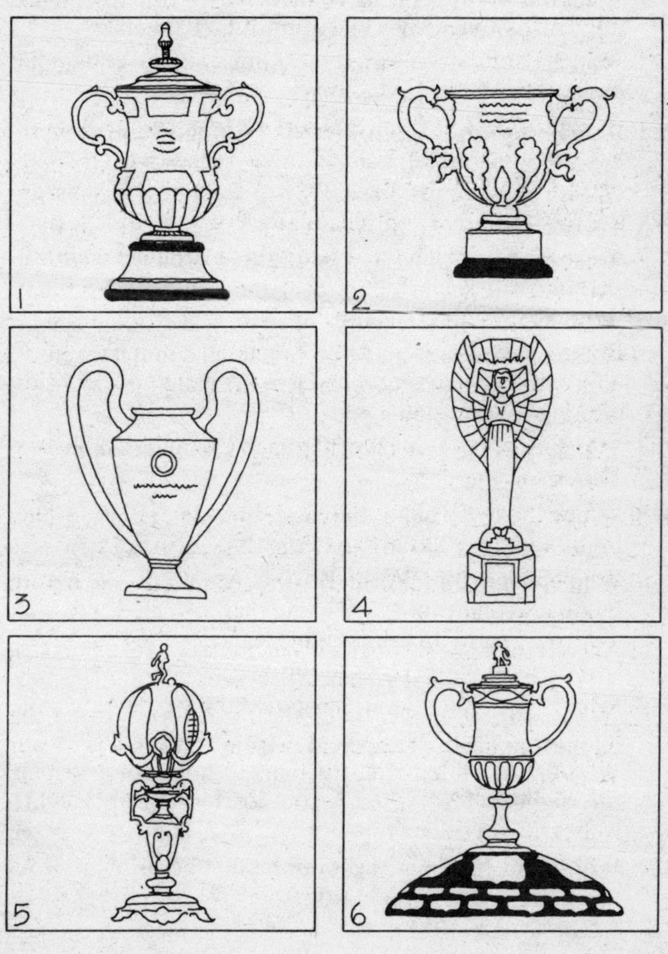

22   Boxing 2

1 Two World Amateur Boxing Champions went on to become World Professional Champions. Can you identify one of them?

2 What odd statistic occurred in the last World title fights involving Dave 'Boy' Green and John Conteh?

3 Who, in 1968, beat Howard Winstone the last time he fought for the World Featherweight title?

4 Who is the only boxer, other than Teofilio Stevenson, to have won Gold Medals at three successive Olympic Games?

5 Terry Downes lost his World Middleweight title in 1962 to the man from whom he had won the title the previous year. Who was his opponent?

6 Alan Minter has recently been World Middleweight Boxing Champion; Tony Sibson is European Middleweight Champion; who is the current *British* Middleweight Champion?

7 Which Briton lost his World title to Charchai Chionoi in 1967?

8 Which boxer gained the first Lonsdale Belt in the Light-welterweight division?

9 Who gained the World Boxing Association's World Featherweight title in 1974, and then switched across to win the World Boxing Council version in 1975 – the first to do so in the modern set-up?

10 Who is the only man to have held the Commonwealth Heavyweight title and the World Heavyweight title?

11 Who finally ended Ken Buchanan's hopes of a British title fight in 1981 when he outpointed him in a light-welterweight title eliminator?

12 Whom did Joe Louis beat on the first occasion he won the World Heavyweight title?

23   Tennis 2

1 Who beat Bjorn Borg 6–0, 6–3 in the 1981 Masters?

2 Who was the first man to win all four major Tournaments – Wimbledon, and the French, American and Australian Championships – though not all in the same year?

3 Rod Laver did not lose any singles matches at Wimbledon between 1960 and 1970: who ended his run of success?

4 Which Champions receive the 'Oxford University Tennis Club Cup' and the 'Sir Herbert Wilberforce Cup'?

5 1980 was a more successful year for Britain than 1981 in the Wightman Cup; at least we won two rubbers. Sue Barker gained one: who won the other?

6 Who were the 1981 holders of the Braniff World Doubles title?

7 Who won the Men's Singles at Wimbledon on the last occasion when the Tournament ran into a third week?

8 Wimbledon 1970 was the only occasion on which Virginia Wade reached the Ladies Doubles Final: who was her partner?

9 Who was the first Briton to appear in a Wimbledon Singles Final after World War II?

10 Who was the first woman to perform the Grand Slam?

11 Who took Bjorn Borg to five sets on the opening day of the 1978 Wimbledon Championships?

12 Bjorn Borg retained his title at the 1980 Masters (held in 1981) and was the first player to do so since 1972–3; who won in those years?

1 Where, in 1923, did England play their last 'home' International at a venue other than Twickenham?

2 Who is the only player to be sent off whilst playing for England in a full International?

3 Which Gloucestershire player scored all his side's points in the 24–9 victory over Middlesex in the 1976 County Championship Final?

4 Who captained England on their first Tour to South Africa in 1972?

5 Why is the 'Calcutta Cup' so called?

6 Where, in 1872, did England play their first International match on home soil?

7 What is the name of the player who scored 17 out of the Overseas XV's 25 points against Wales, in 1980?

8 Which All Black was 'sent off' in the match against Llanelli, and then let off by Alec Hosie, the referee, after discussions with some Llanelli players?

9 Who was the overseas fly-half who played for the South African Barbarians against the 1980 British Lions?

10 The South African rugby touring side is known as the 'Springboks'. What is the name for their Under-24 team?

11 Who kicked the last-minute penalty to give the All Blacks victory in the 1981 series against the Springboks?

12 What is the name of the overseas back row forward who played for the South African Barbarians against the 1980 British Lions?

25   Snooker and Darts

1 Who captained England in the 1980 State Express Snooker World Cup?

2 Cliff Thorburn was World Snooker Champion in 1980: by whom was he beaten in the 1977 Final?

3 Who was the first overseas snooker player to win the 'Pot Black' title?

4 Who was the first winner of the UK Professional Snooker Championships?

5 Whom did Ray Reardon beat in the 1978 World Professional Snooker Championship Final?

6 Who is the only man to have won the Benson and Hedges Snooker Tournament on two occasions?

7 Only two Lancashire men have won the *News of the World* Darts title – in 1948 and 1976. Which of the two won it last?

8 Who is the only overseas darts player to have won the *News of the World* title?

9 Whom did Eric Bristow beat in the 1980 World Darts Championship Final?

10 170 is the highest three dart finish (assuming a double to finish): what is the next highest?

11 Who was the only man to reach the Semi-finals of the 1979, 1980 and 1981 Embassy World Darts Championships?

12 Who finished third in the 1981 World Darts Championships?

1 Which was Geoff Lewis's first Classic winner?

2 Which horse did Edward Hide ride to victory in the 1972 1000-Guineas?

3 What is the name of the horse ridden to victory by G. Thiboeufi in the Oaks in the 1960s?

4 Who was the last Flat-race jockey to ride all six winners on the card?

5 What is the minimum distance for National Hunt races?

6 Who was the last jockey to win the Gold Cup and the Grand National in the same year?

7 Which Scottish race-course was the first to provide a landing strip for aircraft?

8 What was the name of the last horse before Secretariat to win the American Triple Crown?

9 On which course, in 1947, was the first evening meeting held in Britain?

10 On which course did Arkle win his last race?

11 Lester Piggott rode the winner of the St Leger in successive years in the 1960s, and he also rode for the same trainer on both occasions: what is the trainer's name?

12 Doug Smith's Oaks winner in 1969 was Sleeping Partner: who was the jockey?

Grand National

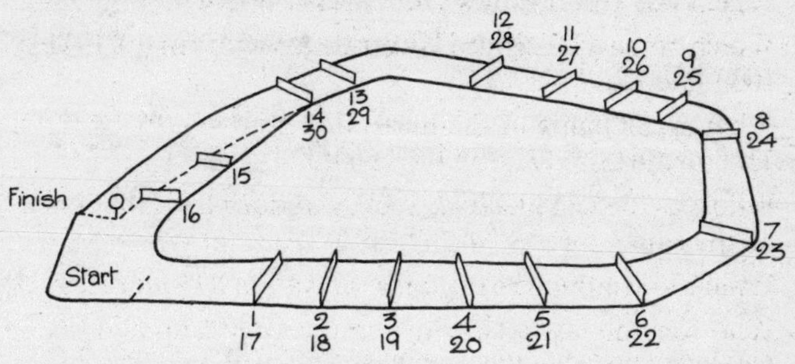

Plan of Aintree race-course. Can you pinpoint: the Canal Turn, Bechers Brook, the Chair, the Water Jump and Valentines?

27   Golf 2

1 Two golf courses have plaques to commemorate great Arnold Palmer shots. Royal Birkdale is one: which is the other?

2 On which course are the last four holes known as Fire Thorn, Red Bud, Nandina and Holly?

3 Where would you find the Eden and Jubilee courses?

4 Britain had two semi-finalists in the 1980 World Match Play Championship for the first time ever. One was Sandy Lyle: who was the other?

5 Which British golfer won the 1980 Australian PGA title?

6 1969 was the only occasion when the Ryder Cup had been tied. On which course did this take place?

7 Which country won the 1980 World Cup Competition?

8 Who was the leading Briton in the 1981 British Open?

9 The winner of the British Open, in addition to receiving a sizeable cheque, also receives a cup. What was presented instead of a cup during the first ten years of the competition?

10 Who, in the 1977 British Open, shot a record round of 63, beating the previous record by two shots?

11 What is the name of the course in the USA designed by Jack Nicklaus?

12 Which golfer holds the unique distinction of having won the British and American Opens in the same year, as well as winning the Amateur titles of those two countries also in the same year?

 Athletics 4

1 Who is the only male athlete to have won four European Games titles?

2 Who won the Olympic 800-Metres title in 1972?

3 Who was the first woman home in the 1981 London Marathon?

4 Which is the only field event won by female athletes from the USA since World War II?

5 Only two British girls finished in the first eight in individual events at the Montreal Olympics. Tessa Sanderson was one: who was the other?

6 In 1964, to whom did the British athlete, Basil Heatley, lose his World 10-Mile record?

7 Roger Bannister ran the first sub-four-minute mile. Who ran the second?

8 How many times did Roger Bannister run a sub-four-minute mile?

9 Who was the last athlete to beat Ed Moses in the 400-Metres Hurdles before 1982?

10 Who was the first man to win the Olympic 110-Metres Hurdles title twice?

11 Who won the famous 1981 *Round the Houses Race* in San Paulo?

12 Which Olympic Champion won the World Cross-Country Championship in 1962, 1967, 1969 and 1972?

29   Boxing 3

1 Which club provided half Britain's six-man team at the 1980 Olympics?

2 Which boxer lost his first fight in twenty professional bouts in 1980, when losing to Matt Saeed Muhammed in a World title fight?

3 Whose unbeaten record of twenty-five fights did Lotte Mwale end in 1978 with a first-round knock-out?

4 Who, in 1974, became the first Nicaraguan-born sportsman to be a World Champion?

5 Which boxer has won a Lonsdale Belt outright in the record period of just six months?

6 Englishmen held the Commonwealth Heavyweight title from June 1958 to July 1972 – who ended that run?

7 Who was the last Briton to suffer a first-round knock-out in a World title fight?

8 What was the Christian name of Henry Cooper's twin brother, also a professional boxer?

9 Who is the only man to have held three different World Boxing titles simultaneously?

10 To whom did Primo Carnera lose his World Heavyweight title?

11 Against whom did John Conteh make his last successful defence of his World title?

12 He fought Ernie Terrell and lost on points for the World Boxing Association title in November 1965; and in March 1966 he lost on points to Muhammed Ali for the World Boxing Council version of the title. What is his name?

Heavyweight Champions

1

(a) Who is it?
(b) Whom did he beat to win the World Heavyweight title for the first time?
(c) Who was the Briton who took him fifteen rounds in a World Heavyweight title fight?

2

(a) Who is it?
(b) What was his nickname?
(c) How many times did he fight in World Heavyweight title fights under his former name?

1 Who played Test cricket against England in 1978 at the age of eighteen?

2 Who was the last wicket-keeper to claim a hundred victims in a season?

3 When Gary Sobers scored his highest Test score of 365 against Pakistan in 1957–8 at Kingston, which West Indian scored 260 in the same innings?

4 Who was the Derbyshire Beneficiary in 1980?

5 Which County finished runners-up for five seasons in succession – four before World War II, and one after?

6 Who has made the highest score in the history of the Gillette Cup Competition?

7 Who was out third ball during the 1980–1 England Tour to the West Indies?

8 Which player made his Test debut for England in the 1980 Centenary Test?

9 In 1961, who, in his final Test match against Australia at the Oval, scored 137 in the first innings?

10 Only two men have won the Man of the Match Award in the Old Gillette Cup final, after finishing on the losing side. Norman Gifford is one: who is the other?

11 Who was England's wicket-keeper, immediately after Godfrey Evans?

12 The second eleven of two First-Class Cricket Counties played in the 1980 Minor Counties Championship; Lancashire was one: which was the other?

1 Which country won its first Winter Olympics Gold Medal at the 1980 Games?

2 Nottinghamshire won the 1981 County Cricket Championship; Torvill and Dean are from Nottingham, Nottingham Forest have won the European Cup; Notts County were promoted to Division 1 – but in which sport did Nottingham Knights win an English Division 2 title in 1980?

3 At the 1980 Moscow Olympics, Russia won the highest number of Gold Medals, with 80; East Germany came second with 47; which country was third, with 8?

4 In which sport was Chris Ronaldson the 1981 World Champion? His wife, Lesley, was the British Open Champion in the same sport: what is it?

5 With which sport would you associate Phil Thomas from Liverpool?

6 Where are the Headquarters of the National Gliding Club?

7 Which Women's World Championships took place on Hayling Island in the summer of 1980?

8 With which sport would you associate the de Montford Centre?

9 Which British ex-Olympic Athletics Champion was elected in 1967 as the first chairman of the British Orienteering Federation?

10 Who beat Terry Griffiths 9–6 to win the 1981 Benson and Hedges Snooker Masters title?

11 Jim Morgan of USA lost his life in 1981 whilst competing in his sport. What sport was this?

12 With which sport would you associate the American Alton Byrd?

32   Soccer 5

1 Which other International captain besides Kevin Keegan joined Hamburg in 1977?

2 Who is Scotland's most capped keeper of all time?

3 Who was the Second Division's leading goal-scorer in 1958, 1959 and 1960?

4 Which football League team once had the quaint name 'Pine Villa'?

5 Which player appeared in the Bolton team in the 1923 and 1926 FA Cup Finals, and also in the 1930 and 1932 Finals – but with Arsenal?

6 What is the better-known name of 'Arthur Artunes Coimbra'?

7 Liverpool have won the European Cup on three occasions, and in a different city each time. They have won it in London and Paris – and in which other city?

8 Joe Jordan went from Manchester United to Italy in 1981: who did the same in 1972?

9 When George Best scored six in the FA Cup win at Northampton – with the score 8–2 – the brother of the Footballer of the Year at that time was in goal for Northampton. What is his name?

10 There is only one Manchester United player with a surname beginning with the letter 'A' who has played for England: who is he?

11 Ted Drake once scored seven goals in a Division 1 match: who were the opposition?

12 In which year was the FA Amateur Cup last contested?

Cup Finals

Eight grounds (excluding replays) have staged the FA Cup Final. Which?

33   Show Jumping

1 Where is the British Show Jumping Derby held?

2 Who won Britain's last Olympic Show Jumping medal?

3 Whom did the British Equestrian Writers name as their 'Young Rider of the Year' for 1980?

4 Who was the 1980 British Equestrian Sports Personality of the year?

5 Who won the 1980 British Show Jumping Derby, beating his brother into second place?

6 Which rider holds the record, before 1982, for wins at Badminton, a record held jointly with Lucinda Prior Palmer?

7 Who won the first Show Jumping World Cup Individual title in 1979?

8 Which horse did Debbie Johnsey ride into fourth place in the Individual Show Jumping event at the 1976 Montreal Olympics?

9 David Broome is still one of the world's leading show jumpers, but in which year did he ride Sunsalve to an Olympic Bronze?

10 What was the name of the horse which collapsed and died whilst being ridden by David Broome in the 1980 Royal Bath and West Show?

11 Which rider would you normally associate with the horse Ryan's Son?

12 Which rider would you normally associate with the horse Buttevant Boy?

1 Honda have won only one Motor-racing Grand Prix, the Mexican, in 1965: who was the American driver?

2 Which former British World Champion switched teams in mid-season?

3 Stirling Moss and Tony Brooks of Great Britain both rode the same car to victory in the 1957 British Grand Prix, after Brooks had handed Moss the car to drive. What was the make of car?

4 Which British girl did rally driver Eric Carlsson marry?

5 Which Briton partnered Jackie Ickx to victory in the 1981 Le Mans 24-hour Race?

6 What was remarkable about Jackie Stewart's win in the 1968 German Grand Prix at the Nurburgring?

7 The RAC Rally has had to be cancelled twice since 1951. The reason in 1957 was petrol rationing: what was the reason in 1967?

8 Which Finn won the RAC Rally in 1973, 1974 and 1975?

9 Which Formula One racing driver won the 1981 Indianapolis 500?

10 Which was James Hunt's last Grand Prix win?

11 Who won the George Medal for pulling Clay Regazzoni out of a blazing car in the 1973 South African Grand Prix?

12 On which race-track in 1962 did Stirling Moss have a near-fatal accident?

Grand Prix Circuits

Each of these countries staged a Formula One Grand Prix in 1981. Name the circuit that was used in each case.

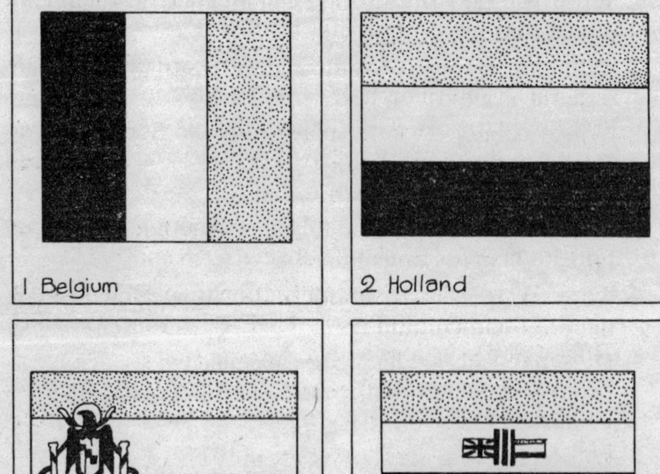

1 Belgium

2 Holland

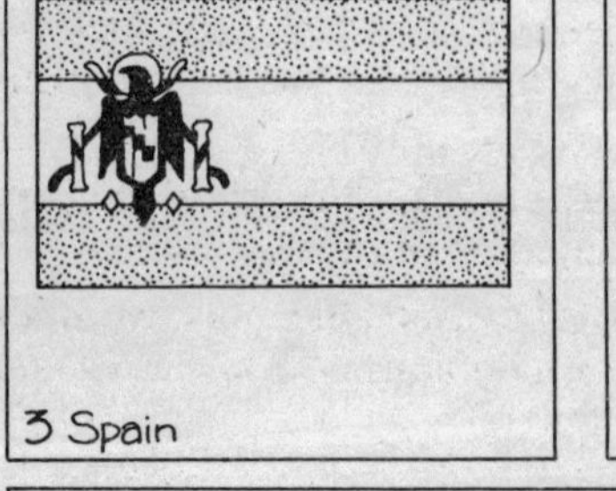

3 Spain

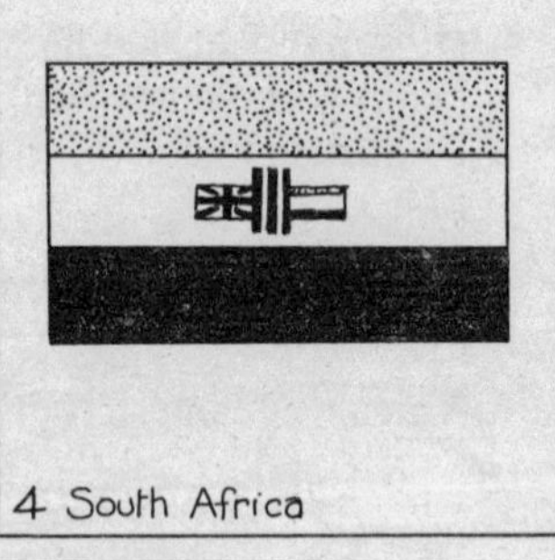

4 South Africa

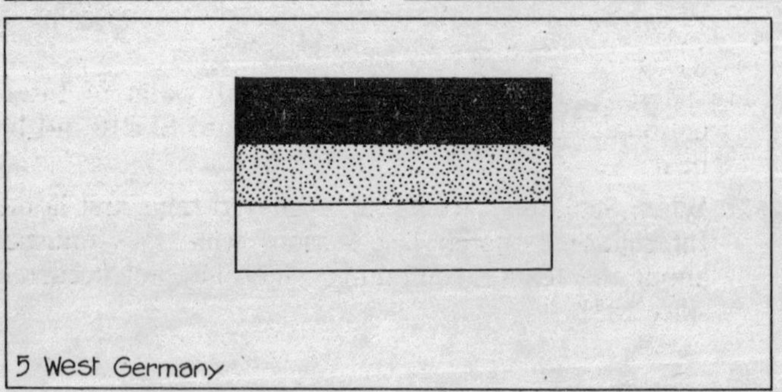

5 West Germany

1 Which club won the 1980–1 Charrington Festival at Twickenham?

2 For which English club did Alan Mexted, brother of All Black Murray Mexted, play in 1980–1?

3 Who, in 1981, equalled the World record of three drop goals in an International?

4 Which county cricketer played for the South African Barbarians against British Lions in 1974 and scored twelve of their sixteen points?

5 What is the name of the full-back who made nineteen appearances for England between 1968 and 1972?

6 Tony Ward, the Irish International, played football against Southampton in the UEFA Cup, but for which Rugby club side does he play?

7 What is the name of the Springbok who captained his country in two 1981 series, and was in fact captain in his first Test?

8 From whom did Fergus Slattery take the title of the Irish flanker with the highest number of caps?

9 Since the start of the Scots Division One, only two clubs up to 1982 have won the Championship. Hawick is one: what is the name of the other?

10 Which county won the Thorn County Championship in 1981 – for the first time since 1898?

11 When Andy Irvine scored his 213th point in International Rugby in 1981, whose record of 210 did he beat?

12 When Scotland's Rugby team played their first home International match last season, what was unusual about the team – something which has not occurred since 1881?

1 Who, in 1979, took what was then a record 73 Test wickets – in a calendar year?

2 In the Tied Test of 1960, which Australian took 11 wickets?

3 Who was the last First-Class cricketer to score 300 runs in an innings on two occasions?

4 Who was the last Australian to score a century on his Test debut – before Dirk Wellham in 1981?

5 Which County cricket captain was born in Venezuela?

6 Which ground was awarded, and then had a 1981 one-day Test match taken away?

7 Which brothers were both in the Top Twenty of the 1980 First-Class bowling averages?

8 Which former World Boxing Champion's son went on the England Under-19 Cricket Tour in 1980–1?

9 Who was the oldest cricketer to play on the 1981 England Tour to the West Indies?

10 Which was the last of the seventeen First-Class Counties to join the County Championship – in 1921?

11 Which County did not bowl a single ball in First-Class cricket during May 1981?

12 Who was the last Lancashire cricketer to score a Test century at Old Trafford?

37   Swimming

1 Which Briton finished second in the Men's 200-Metres Butterfly event at the 1980 Olympics and became Britain's first medallist of the Games?

2 Which young American girl swimmer won five gold Medals at the 1978 World Championships?

3 Who won the Men's two Individual Medley titles at the 1968 Olympics?

4 The only swimming Gold Medal won by the host nation at the 1968 Olympics was in the Men's 200-Metres Breast Stroke: who was the winner?

5 The 200-Metres Freestyle for Men was reintroduced into the Olympic swimming programme in 1968: who won the title on that occasion?

6 The Women's 200-Metres Freestyle was first contested at the 1968 Olympics and was won by a swimmer who, at the same Games, also won the first-ever Women's 800 Metres Freestyle. What was her name?

7 At the 1976 Montreal Olympics, which male swimmer represented Britain in the Finals of both the 4 × 100 Medley Relay, and the 4 × 200 Freestyle Relay?

8 In the Water Polo event, which country has won a medal at every Olympic Games since 1928?

9 Who was the first man to win four Gold Medals at the Olympic Games in the one year?

10 Bobby McGregor won four major Silver Medals and broke five World Records, but where did he win his only major title?

11 Which girl won Britain's first post-war Swimming Olympic Gold Medal?

12 Who won both the Women's Individual Medley races at the 1968 Olympics?

38   Soccer 6

1 At the end of the 1981–2 season, who is the Chairman of the Professional Footballers Association?

2 Two Football League players have taken part in European Cup Finals for different clubs. One is Kevin Keegan: who is the other?

3 Arsenal's record win and loss against the same club – now no longer in the Football League. What is the name of this club?

4 Who were known as 'Smash and Grab'?

5 Which present-day First Division side was formerly known as 'St Luke's'?

6 Whom did Ipswich Town beat – against all the odds – in the Semi-final of the 1980–81 UEFA Cup?

7 Which club did Ted McDougall join from Manchester United?

8 Which is the only present-day Alliance Premier League side to have played in the Football League?

9 In the 1980–1 season, who were the only First Division side to score six goals in one match in the Football League?

10 Who refereed the 1950 World Cup Final?

11 From which club did Preston North End sign Tommy Docherty as a player?

12 Who scored a hat-trick in the 1980 European Championship Finals in Italy?

World Cup, World Cup

Nine members of the England team that went to the World Cup Finals in Chile in 1962 were in the squad for the 1966 competition. Who were they?

1 Which international tennis tournament takes place each year in an Olympic complex?

2 Name the last man to retain his Men's Singles title at Wimbledon before Bjorn Borg.

3 Who in 1971 was the first winner of the WLT Championship – a title he retained the following year?

4 From whom did Ilie Nastase, the number one seed at the 1973 Wimbledon Championships, receive what was then a shock defeat?

5 Who is the only man to have won the Men's Singles Title six years in succession at Wimbledon?

6 Who was the only player to beat Bjorn Borg twice in 1980?

7 Who has made the greatest number of Davis Cup appearances for Great Britain?

8 Who was the last British girl before Ann Jones to win the Ladies' Singles at Wimbledon?

9 Who, in 1976, was the last British Men's tennis player before Buster Mottram to reach the last sixteen of the US Open?

10 Bjorn Borg won Wimbledon in 1980: which 1980 Open did Mrs Borg win?

11 Which unseeded player reached the Semi-finals of the 1980 Wimbledon Men's Singles?

12 Who won the Men's Singles in the first Grand Slam event of 1981 – the Australian Open?

1 Which is the only one of the Queen's horses to have finished in the first three in the Derby?

2 Who owned the 1980 Caesarewitch winner Popsi's Joy? He also owned the winner in 1974, and rode a winner at the age of sixty-seven.

3 Who was Hyperion's jockey in all his races?

4 Before 1981, which was the last horse to win the following races in the same season: the King George VI and Queen Elizabeth Diamond Stakes, and the *Prix de l'Arc de Triomphe*?

5 In 1963, Mill House became the first horse to beat Arkle in a steeplechase: what was the race?

6 Which was the first horse to beat Shergar?

7 Name the last horse, before Nijinsky, to win three English Classics in one season.

8 Which horse, a former winner of the Washington DC International, was afterwards taken into training with Fred Winter?

9 In 1981, who trained the winners of the English and French 2000-Guineas?

10 Who trained a treble at Worcester on 3 January 1981, with Fort Belvedere, Bueche Giorod and Roll of Drums – and achieved a major breakthrough?

11 Scobie Breasley's second Derby win was on Charlotte-town, in 1966: who was the trainer?

12 The 1974 Derby was won by Snow Night: who was the trainer?

41   Athletics 5

1 Which Briton finished seventh in the Men's 400-Metres at the Montreal Olympics?

2 Who is the youngest male athlete to compete for Britain in a full Senior International?

3 Two World 5000-Metres records were broken on the same day on the same track in Norway in 1981. Henry Rono broke his own world record; which girl set a new world mark for the distance in her race?

4 Which French girl beat the late Lillian Board into second place in the 400-Metres Final at the 1968 Olympics?

5 Which British athlete reached the Men's 400-Metres Hurdles Final at the 1976 Montreal Olympics?

6 Who is the reigning Olympic Long Jump record holder?

7 Who won Britain's only track athletics medal at the 1976 Montreal Olympics?

8 Who won Britain's first track Gold Medal at the Olympic Games since 1932 when he won a Gold at the 1956 Games?

9 Who won the 1980 *Golden Mile* at Crystal Palace?

10 Who was Britain's first pole vaulter to clear 18 foot?

11 Who won the 1981 *Bannister Mile*?

12 Britain had four Gold Medallists in the 1981 European Cup Final. Three of them were Coe, Ovett and Moorcroft: who was the fourth?

Fill in the blanks

The blanks in each of the following post-war Olympic Finals reveal the name of a British Medallist: who are they?

1956 Men's 800-Metres

1 Thomas Courtney (USA)
2 ?   ?   ?
3 Auden Boysen (Norway)

1964 Marathon

1 Abebe Bikila (Ethiopia)
2 ?   ?   ?
3 Kokichi Tsuburaya (Japan)

1960 Men's 100-Metres

1 Armin Hary (Germany)
2 Dave Sime (USA)
3 ?   ?   ?

1972 Men's 1500-Metres

1 Lasse Viren (Finland)
2 Mohamed Gamoudi (Tunisia)
3 ?   ?   ?

1968 Men's 400-Metres Hurdles

1 ?   ?   ?
2 Gerhard Hennige (West Germany)
3 ?   ?   ?

1952 3000-Metres Steeplechase

1 Horace Ashenfelter (USA)
2 Vlademir Kazantsev (USSR)
3 ?   ?   ?

1 Who became the first golfer in 1980 to win over half a million dollars in prize money in one year?

2 Who won the Individual title at the 1980 Eisenhower Trophy?

3 Who finished as runner-up to Tony Jacklin in the year he won the British Open?

4 Whom did Sandy Lyle beat by just £278 when he won the 1980 Order of Merit and Harry Vardon Trophy?

5 Who won the 1980 European Open Golf title?

6 Which Briton did Greg Norman beat in the Final of the 1980 Suntory World Match Play Championship at Wentworth?

7 On which course did Great Britain and Northern Ireland last win the Ryder Cup, in 1957?

8 Who is the only Briton to have won the Individual title in the World Cup Competition?

9 In which county is the Royal St George's course, the venue of the 1981 British Open?

10 Who was the last man to win the British Open two years in succession?

11 Which Briton finished equal second with Johnny Miller, behind Tom Weiskopf, in the 1973 British Open?

12 Who, in 1978, shot a round of 111 in the Italian Open – the highest score ever recorded in a Professional tournament?

43   Boxing 4

1 Two boxers won their third World title in 1981. One was Arguello: who was the other?

2 Who was voted the best young British boxer of 1980 by the Boxing Writers' Club?

3 Britain has had four European Middleweight Champions since 1974. Three of them are Sibson, Minter and Kevin Finnegan: who is the fourth?

4 The first-ever World Heavyweight title fight between two negro boxers took place in 1939. Joe Louis was one: who was the other?

5 Whose real name was Joseph Barrow?

6 Give the names of the following two boxers: one held the World Featherweight title in 1969, and the other, his uncle, fought Willie Pep for the same title in 1950.

7 Who was the first man to defeat Jim Watt *in* Scotland?

8 In Dick Tiger's six World Middleweight title fights, what was the name of the man who provided the opposition in three of the fights – in which Tiger won two, and drew one?

9 A former British Featherweight Champion he had his last fight in 1945 at the age of thirty-nine and successfully defended his title. This was quite remarkable for a man who had only one good lung: what is this boxer's name?

10 Whom did Jimmy Ellis beat on points in April 1968 to take the World Boxing Association version of the World Heavyweight title?

11 Which former British Heavyweight Champion had his last fight in 1953, at the age of thirty-nine, against Don Cockell?

12 Who was the only man to lose to both Muhammed Ali and Floyd Patterson in World title fights?

1 Which player made his hundredth appearance in an All Black jersey in the 1980 Centenary match against Wales?

2 Who was the only member of the British Lions party touring New Zealand in 1966 to tour the same country with them again in 1977?

3 Who captained the All Blacks on the 1972 Tour to the British Isles?

4 Leicester have letters instead of numbers on their shirts. What letter does Dusty Hare, the full-back, wear on his shirt?

5 Who were Richmond playing when the Chris Ralston affair hit the headlines in 1979?

6 Which team won the John Player Cup in 1981 for the third successive year?

7 What Rugby Union team was founded in Bradford in 1890 by Percy Carpmael?

8 Which 1980 British Lions player lasted only forty-seven seconds on the Tour to South Africa?

9 Which Rugby club, now defunct, won the Middlesex Sevens in 1957, and again in 1969?

10 Which team has won the Hospitals Cup on a record thirty occasions?

11 What was noteworthy, in a rugby context, about the 1980 University Rugby captains?

12 Which team was beaten 4–0 by the village club Penclawdd in the first round of the 1980–1 Welsh Rugby Union Cup?

Rugby Union Caps

Can you identify the nine players who, at the start of the 1981–2 season, had won fifty or moré caps for their country – Lions Caps excluded?

45   General 5

1 Which sport, in addition to Lawn Tennis, is included in the full title of the All England Club?

2 How many players are there in a Volleyball team?

3 Soccer has its kick-off: how do the players start a Basketball match?

4 Of which sport are FISA and FOCA the two governing bodies?

5 Who is the 1981 World Men's Figure-Skating Champion?

6 What is the maximum score which can be 'rolled' in one frame in a game of Ten-pin Bowling?

7 Which World Championships of 1981 were held in Novi Sad, in Serbia?

8 In an America's Cup Race in 1980, Australia beat *Freedom*: this was the first US defeat since 1970. Which Australian boat won in that year?

9 Who is the 1981 World Women's Figure-Skating Champion?

10 A British girl led the field in the 1981 European Figure-Skating Championships. She went into the final round, but a series of disasters resulted in her gaining only sixth place: who is she?

11 Which country won the Badminton Uber Cup between 1956 to 1965?

12 Which Football League Club has a team in the National Basketball League of the same name in the 1981–2 season?

1 Which was the last club to be promoted to Division 1 after failing to reach promotion in the usual way, i.e. from first or second place in Division 2?

2 Which is the minimum sum that an away team is assured out of the gate-money at a Football League match?

3 Whom did Newcastle United beat 13–0 in a Second Division game in 1946?

4 Who captained the successful Cardiff City side which won the FA Cup in 1927 and became the first side to take the trophy out of England?

5 Three of Argentina's World Cup-winning squad have played in the Football League: Ardiles, Villa, and who else?

6 Who were the last brothers to win FA Cup-winners Medals in the same match?

7 From which Argentinian club was Osvaldo Ardiles signed?

8 Who, in 1980, was manager of both of the two deadly rivals, Hearts and Hibernians, within three months' space?

9 Who are the reigning Olympic Soccer Champions?

10 With which Football League club did Bill Shankly start his playing career?

11 Which was the last club to be relegated from Division 1 and then immediately promoted again?

12 By which non-League side were Leicester City knocked out of the FA Cup in 1979–80, the year in which they were promoted into Division 1?

Football League Clubs

The map shows ten seaside resorts. Can you identify the
Football League clubs nearest to each of the towns?

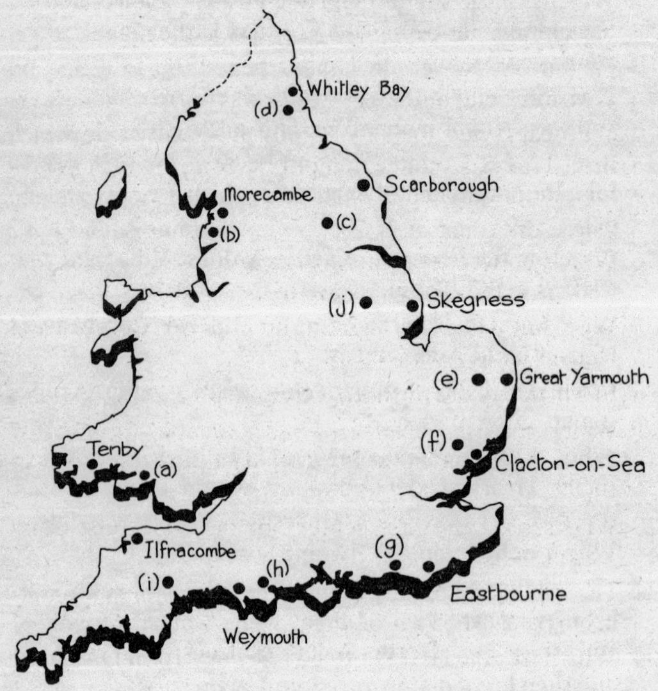

1 Which club uses Lords in September after Middlesex?

2 When Bobby Simpson scored his 311 for Australia against England at Old Trafford in 1964, which Englishman scored 256 in the same match?

3 Which man has captained England to the highest number of wins – 20?

4 Which Australian Test cricketer was born in Yugoslavia and changed his name from 'Durtanovitch'?

5 Fred Trueman made a temporary come-back in 1972 – for one-day matches only. For which County did he play?

6 Which bowler took more than a thousand First-Class wickets in the 1950s and also in the 1960s?

7 Who has won the highest number of Benson and Hedges Gold Awards?

8 In which city did the Tied Test take place?

9 Which English batsman scored a century on his Test debut, when playing at Lords against the West Indies in 1969?

10 Who scored the first century of the 1981 First-Class season?

11 Three players scored centuries on their major County debut in 1981. Two of them were Martyn Moxon of Yorkshire and Derek Aslett of Kent: who was the third?

12 Who, in 1962, became the youngest man to score a Test century in England?

1 Dick Hern established a new record in 1980 for First Prize money won in a season, when his stable amassed £830,000. This amount beat the previous record, set in 1979, by almost £150,000. What is the name of the trainer who set this record?

2 Which race was permanently transferred from Manchester to Doncaster in 1964?

3 Stan Mellor has ridden over a thousand National Hunt winners: who is next on the all-time list?

4 Who rode the winner of the US Derby in 1955, 1959 and 1965?

5 On which course is the Lockinge Stakes normally run?

6 Which horse won the 1981 German and Italian Derbys, and was second in our own Derby?

7 Tommy Carmody has ridden the last three winners of the King George Steeplechase at Kempton. In 1979 and 1980 he rode Silver Buck: on which horse did he win the race in 1978?

8 Which horse was voted 1980 Racehorse of the Year?

9 Lester Piggott rejoined Henry Cecil at Warren Place in 1981 for the first time since his spell at Warren Place from 1954 to 1966. Whom did he replace in 1954?

10 Who was the last trainer, before Dick Hern in 1980, to train the winners of the Derby and the Oaks in the same season?

11 What was the name of the horse ridden by Ron Barry when he won the Cheltenham Gold Cup?

12 What is a 'chalk' jockey?

49   Motor Racing 2

1 France has a proud history of Grand Prix racing: which French driver has won the highest number of Grands Prix under the modern set-up since 1950?

2 Who, in 1980, was the first Briton since Mike Hailwood in 1972 to win the European Formula Two Championship?

3 Which Formula One Grand Prix is held on the Kayalami circuit?

4 Which firm offered Jackie Stewart over a million pounds in 1979 to return to Grand Prix racing?

5 Who was the first driver to win both US Grands Prix in the same year?

6 Only two British drivers gained points in the 1980 World Championship, and both were Irish. Tom Watson was one: who was the other?

7 Who was the only driver, besides John Watson, to have won his own country's Grand Prix in 1981?

8 Which country, in 1981, had the highest number of Grand Prix drivers who were currently racing in that year's World Championship?

9 Who was Jacques Laffite's team-mate with Ligier in 1981?

10 Which Brazilian won the 1980 Dutch Grand Prix?

11 Which Briton drove for the Lotus Formula One Motor-racing team in 1981?

12 Who is the only driver to have won a Grand Prix in his very first race?

Where Are They?

Can you identify these motor racing circuits?

1 Situated two hundred and sixty miles north of New York City, it is 3.38 miles in length.

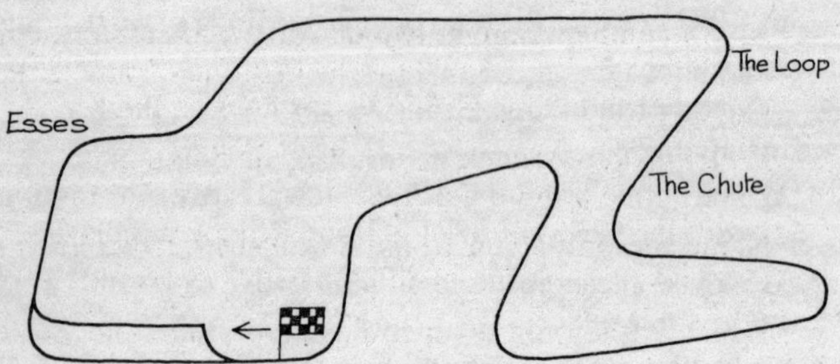

2 2.06 miles in length, it is the slowest circuit Grand Prix.

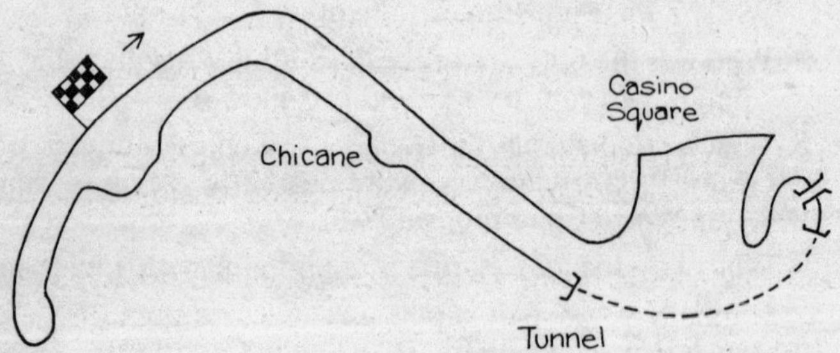

3 Twenty miles south-west of London, it is 2.64 miles long.

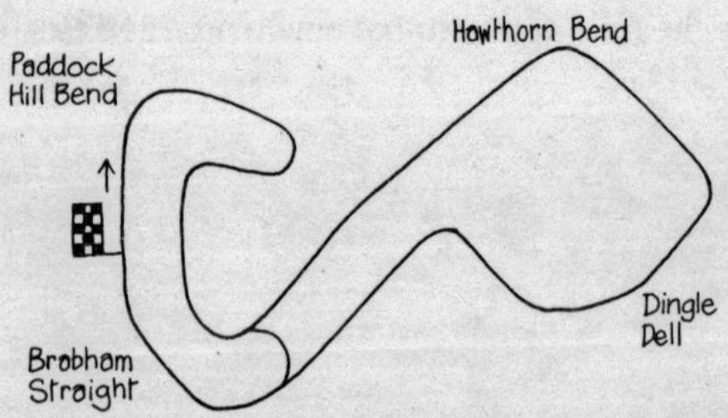

1 Which was the first team to win the Rugby League Challenge Cup on five occasions?

2 Which two players shared the Lance Todd Award in the 1965 Final between Wigan and Hunslet?

3 In 1980 Fulham bought two players from the same club and paid a fee of £25,000 for the first time. Name either player.

4 Which Rugby League team plays its home matches at Lawkholme Lane?

5 Name the only team to have won the Challenge Cup Final two years in succession on two occasions.

6 Which is the only team to have won the John Player Trophy on three occasions?

7 For which Rugby League team did Arthur Rowe, the British Shot Put Champion, sign in 1962?

8 In 1971–2, who were the first winners of the John Player Trophy?

9 Steve Hesford, in 1980, became only the second man to kick five hundred goals in the First Division. Who was the first?

10 Which was the first Rugby League club officially to beat Fulham at Craven Cottage in league competition?

11 Who is the only man to have won the Lance Todd Award twice?

12 Which player holds the record in making 921 first class Rugby League appearances between 1921 and 1946?

1   Which player won all three available titles in his one and only Wimbledon?

2   Who was the fourth seed beaten by John Lloyd in the first round of the 1977 Wimbledon Championships?

3   In the Men's Singles at the 1981 Wimbledon Championships, who was the first male seed to be knocked out?

4   Butch Bucholz is one of the game's top administrators, but what was his unique achievement in 1958?

5   Bjorn Borg won his fifth French Open title in 1980: whose previous record of four wins did he beat?

6   Where did Borg lose two penalties for arguing – the only occasion on which this has happened?

7   Virginia Wade has made the highest number of Wightman Cup appearances for Britain. Who is the runner-up?

8   What was the score in the most famous of all tie-breaks – the Borg-McEnroe Wimbledon Final of 1980?

9   Bobby Wilson and Mike Davies reached the 1960 Wimbledon Doubles Final. By whom were they beaten?

10 Which man was left out of the British Rankings in 1981 – for the first time since 1968?

11 Who was the youngest male competitor at the 1981 Wimbledon Championships?

12 Who was the last men's number one seed at Wimbledon before Bjorn Borg monopolised the position?

1 Who scored the first Test century ever made in Antigua?

2 Before 1982, only two players, not test players, had scored 2000 runs in a season since the Championship reduction. One is Roy Virgin: who is the other?

3 Who was the first Indian cricketer to take 1500 wickets in his career?

4 Who topped the England bowling averages against Australia in summer 1981?

5 Name the cricketer who played in fifty-eight Tests between 1972 and 1977 which were not only consecutive but comprised his entire Test career?

6 Which batsman topped England's batting averages in the 1981 Series against Australia with an average of 59.33?

7 Pakistan have the youngest-ever Test cricketer in Mushtaq; they also have the second-youngest. What is his name?

8 Who won the 1981 Australian Gillette Cup?

9 Who captained Yorkshire to six Championships during his nine years in charge?

10 Which is the only County to have lost twice to University sides in the Benson and Hedges Cup?

11 Which cricket Final did Hampshire reach in 1980?

12 Namc two of thc thrcc Young Cricketers on the Whitbread scheme to Australia in 1980–1.

Cricket Champions

Fill in the missing Champions of the 1970s:

County Championship		*Gillette Cup*
Kent	1970	Lancashire
Surrey	1971	? ? ?
Warwickshire	1972	Lancashire
Hampshire	1973	Gloucestershire
Worcestershire	1974	Kent
? ? ?	1975	Lancashire
Middlesex	1976	Northamptonshire
? ? ?	1977	Middlesex
Kent	1978	? ? ?
Essex	1979	Somerset

John Player		*Benson & Hedges*
Lancashire	1970	(not competed)
Worcestershire	1971	(not competed)
Kent	1972	Leicestershire
? ? ?	1973	Kent
Leicestershire	1974	? ? ?
Hampshire	1975	Leicestershire
Kent	1976	Kent
Leicestershire	1977	? ? ?
Hampshire	1978	Kent
? ? '?	1979	Essex

1 Who are the reigning Olympic Polo Champions?

2 At which resort did Robin Nash and Tony Dixon win their Bobsleighing Olympic Gold Medal?

3 Which oarsman has won a record six Head Of The River races?

4 Which World Champion is the husband of Olympic Champion Anita Lonsborough?

5 Of which sporting event of 1981 was Ronnie Howard the Umpire?

6 About ten years ago, Snooker Plus was tried as an experiment. Two additional colours were used, one being orange: what was the other?

7 Who won the 1980 World Masters Squash title at Wembley?

8 In which sport are Teresa Burton, of Lewisham, and Steve Sowerby, of Harrogate, reigning British Champions?

9 Who overtook Peter Sprogis's British Basketball League record of 2143 points in November 1980?

10 On which Greyhound track is the 'Laurels' normally run?

11 Which British International retired in 1981 after 415 appearances for England over a period of twenty-three years?

12 With which sport would you associate the Brinnington Lapwings Ladies team?

54 Horse Racing 5

1 When Sea Pigeon, in 1980, won his sixteenth race at Ayr, which horse's Flat-race gelding prize money record did he beat?

2 Which race-course in England is furthest south?

3 Who is Glint of Gold's regular jockey?

4 At the end of the 1981 season, which jockey holds the record for riding the highest number of English Classics in a career (27)?

5 In 1970, which horse was put down with advanced arthritis in Derby week?

6 Who, in winning the Lincolnshire Handicap in 1957 and 1971, became the only current jockey to have ridden the winner of the race at its original course in Lincoln and also at its present home at Doncaster?

7 Name the horse who finished fourth in the 1981 Cheltenham Gold Cup, and started favourite for the 1981 Grand National.

8 Two jockeys both rode their first English Classic winners in 1975: name either of them.

9 Who rode Vincent O'Brien's first Derby winner, Larkspur?

10 Walter Swinburn rode for the Michael Stoute stable in 1981; to which trainer was he apprenticed in 1980?

11 Who is the only National Hunt jockey to have ridden a century of winners in successive seasons?

12 In which major 1980 race did To-Agori-Mou lose to the ill-fated Storm Bird?

1 Which club has the worst disciplinary record, pro-rata, in the Football League?

2 From which club did Don Revie join Leeds United as a player?

3 Eamonn Collins of Blackpool is the youngest player (14 years 323 days) to play for a League club in a competitive match; against whom was the match played?

4 Colin Lee, ex-Torquay, scored four goals for Spurs during their 9–0 win in 1977; against whom was the match played?

5 Which club, between 1922 and 1927, finished as runners-up in the Third Division South for six years in succession?

6 Which current Football League International has a brother who plays alongside him in his national team's defence?'

7 Who was the last Leeds United player to win the Football Writers' 'Player of the Year' Award?

8 In 1980–1, which First Division club lost a match 7–1 to a Second Division club?

9 Who was the Football League's fourth 'million pound' player – after Francis, Daly and Gray?

10 Which Third Division footballer played for England in 1976?

11 Which was the first team to win the First Division title and the Football League Cup in the same season?

12 Who was the coach to the Great Britain Olympic team in 1952?

Travellin' Light

Here are four much-travelled Football League players, and the clubs that they played for, in order. Can you name the players and fill in the gaps?

Portsmouth
Blackburn Rovers
? ? ?
Peterborough United
Leicester City
Wolverhampton Wanderers

Bradford City
Nottingham Forest
Newcastle United
Birmingham City
? ? ?
Norwich City
Aston Villa
Bradford City

Leicester City
Rotherham United
Carlisle United
Wolverhampton Wanderers
Bristol City
? ? ?
Middlesborough
Preston North End
Carlisle United

Notts County
Aston Villa
? ? ?
Liverpool
Coventry City
Birmingham City
Notts County
Oldham Athletic

1 Which County cricketer has captained the Australian Under-19 Team against England?

2 Who, in 1981, at the age of fifteen, was the youngest cricketer to be given a professional contract?

3 Which bowler resigned in the middle of a 1980 Test Series because he said that the wickets were badly prepared?

4 Who won the inaugural Lambert and Butler Floodlight Cricket Cup?

5 Who are the only father and son to have won Benson and Hedges Cup Winners' Medals?

6 Who captained South Africa in their last official Test Match in 1970?

7 Wellham, Border, Yallop and another Australian cricketer scored Test centuries in the memorable series against England in 1981. Who was the other player?

8 Who, in 1963, was the last man to win the Young Cricketer of the Year Award, and play in a County Championship winning side in the same year?

9 Which player, before Geoff Boycott, held the record for scoring the highest number of Test *half*-centuries?

10 Which Third Division football ground hosted group matches of the Lambert and Butler Floodlight Cricket Cup?

11 In the history of Test cricket, who has been captain on the greatest number of occasions?

12 By how many points did Nottinghamshire win the 1981 County Championship from Sussex?

57   Golf 4

1 At the 1981 British Open, who shot a course record 65, including a hole in one? The same player, a few years previously, was a third cornet-player in the Hammond Sauce Band!

2 Which of the World's four leading Tournaments was the last one introduced – in 1934?

3 Which course staged the very first British Open in 1860?

4 Who were the very first winners of the Canada Cup, now known as the World Cup?

5 Who was chairman of the Royal and Ancient in 1971, the year in which Britain won the Walker Cup at St Andrews?

6 Who won the 1980 British Women's Order of Merit?

7 In 1972, who was the first non-American to win a million dollars on the US golf circuit?

8 Who were runners-up to Canada in the 1980 Golf World Cup?

9 Which European golfer won the 1976 Dunlop Masters title?

10 Three Australians have won the World Matchplay title in the past seven years. Two are Greg Norman and Graham Marsh: who is the third?

11 Who was the first golfer to be on the winning team in three consecutive World Cups?

12 Who was the 1980 British Women's Match Play Champion?

1 How many players are there in a Basketball team?

2 Who made a new record break of 127 at the 1980 World Amateur Snooker Championships?

3 With which sport would you associate Graham Noyce?

4 Who, in reaching the Men's Singles Final at the 1977 English Open Table Tennis Championships, became the first English player to do so since 1960?

5 Which 1978 Greyhound Derby winner finished second in the 1979 race?

6 Which reigning World Pool Champion frequently enters Snooker events?

7 Who is the reigning World Coach and Fours Driving Champion?

8 How many players are there in a Polo team?

9 On which Soccer ground in 1981 did England play two Hockey Internationals – against Holland and West Germany?

10 For which sport is the W. K. Lennard Trophy awarded?

11 Who is regarded as the founder of the modern Olympic Games?

12 Who was the only American to win an Individual Olympic Gold Medal in 1980?

Which Game?

Six balls which are used in seven different sports: cricket, lawn tennis, soccer, polo, table tennis, water polo and hockey. Can you identify them?

Maximum Circumference

1   28"

2   10.21"

3   9.25"

4   9"

5   8.25"

6   4.71"

1 Which series of races took place at Meadowlands?

2 On which race-course does the annual Flat-racing season traditionally open in England?

3 Which is the only Irish-trained horse to have won the Washington DC International?

4 Name the British race-course which stages the highest number of racing days in a calendar year?

5 The winner of the 1980 Lambert Premier Chase Final was Royal Bond, trained by Arthur Moore, whose father had trained the first winner of the race ten years previously; the race was then called the Wills Premier Chase. What was the name of this horse?

6 Who was the last man before Peter Easterby, in 1981, to train the winner of both the Cheltenham Gold Cup and the Champion Hurdle in the same season?

7 Who was the last man before Don McCain to train successive Grand National winners?

8 Which race course is called 'The Roodee'?

9 Who rode Sea Pigeon to his very first victory – at Ascot – in 1972?

10 What is the name of the last filly to win the St Leger?

11 Who was the 1980 Irish Flat-race Champion Jockey?

12 In 1980, Detroit provided Robert Sangster with his third *Prix de L'Arc de Triomphe* winner; which horse provided his other two victories?

1 Geoff Boycott has opened the England batting with three men who have captained England in Test cricket: two of them are Mike Brearley and Colin Cowdrey. Who is the third?

2 Which is the only County to have appeared in three successive Benson and Hedges Cup Finals?

3 Up to 1981, which County finished second, first, second and second in the last four John Player Leagues?

4 Which bowler took 7–12 and 6–17 in the 1978 Benson and Hedges games?

5 Who, in 1980, was the last cricketer (and probably the first!) to win his County cap without playing a County game?

6 Who holds the record for scoring the highest number of First-class centuries?

7 Who was the last cricketer to amass career statistics of 20,000 runs and 2000 wickets?

8 The double is an almost forgotten feat nowadays in cricket: which player was the last to gain the double of 2000 runs and 100 wickets in a season?

9 Which England cricketer has a brother who plays regular First Division football?

10 Who, in 1977–8 was the last man before Dirk Wellham to score a century on his Test debut?

11 Who is the only cricketer to have won Benson and Hedges Winners' Medals with two different Counties?

12 Who is the only man besides Viv Richards to have won the 'Man of the Match' Award in both the Gillette Cup Final and the Benson and Hedges Cup Final?

61   Soccer 9

1 Which club has obtained the greatest number of points
in the First Division without winning the title prior to
1981–2?

2 Which Canadian-born player appeared in the 1977 and
1979 FA Cup Finals?

3 Keith Burkinshaw was manager of the Spurs team
which won the FA Cup in 1981; in the 1970s he was the
coach to a team which was beaten in the Final. What
is the name of the latter team?

4 Which was the last club to win the FA Cup for the first
time?

5 Who wore the number nine shirt for Manchester United
in their victory over Benfica in the European Cup Final?

6 Which Paris daily newspaper was responsible for the
introduction of the European Cup in 1955?

7 Which club was replaced in the Football League by
Cambridge United?

8 Which 'million pound' player, at the age of twenty-one,
has already played under ten managers?

9 For which League club did Jimmy Greaves's son Danny
play in 1981?

10 Which is the only Yugoslav club to have won a major
European Trophy?

11 By whom was the highest number of goals (13) scored in
the Final rounds of one World Cup?

12 Two present-day Football League teams have won the
FA Amateur Cup. One is Wimbledon: what is the name
of the other?

Answers

1   1982 Elimination Round

1 Nottingham Forest.
2 Kirov (USSR).
3 Govind.
4 France.
5 St Andrews.
6 Hana Mandlikova.
7 Charlton Athletic.
8 Lester Piggott.
9 Bobsleigh (2-man Bob).
10 Roy Gumbs (Middleweight).
11 Cliff Thorburn.
12 John Surtees.
13 Telford United.
14 Phil Neale.
15 Don Thompson (Walk).
16 Bill Beaumont.
17 McMillan and Stove (Mixed Doubles).
18 1951.
19 Jocky Wilson.
20 Brisbane.
21 Ripon and Redcar.
22 Dwight Davison.
23 Steve Fenwick (Cardiff).
24 Alain Prost.
25 Diego Maradona.
26 Bruce Jenner.
27 South Africa.
28 Davey Moore (Light-middleweight).
29 Swimming.
30 Graham Marsh.
31 Bill Beaumont and Willie Carson.
32 Darts.
33 Nicklaus Silver.
34 Mike Weaver.

35 Harry Mallin.
36 Niki Lauda.
37 Swansea.
38 Harold Abrahams.
39 Eric Liddell.
40 Ciaran Fitzgerald (Ireland).
41 Scott Hamilton (USA).
42 Evonne Cawley (nee Goolagong).
43 Vladimir Salnikov (USSR).
44 Cardiff.
45 Aldaniti.
46 Ken Buchanan.
47 Syd Millar.
48 West Ham, White City and Hackney.
49 Cska Sofia.
50 June Croft.
51 Wilf Slack.
52 Alan Brazil (Ipswich).
53 Christine Truman.
54 Peter Tupling.
55 Crystal Palace.
56 Gordon Richards.
57 Alexis Arguello.
58 Grand Prix motor cars.
59 Hungary.
60 Paul Parker.
61 Nadia Comeneci.
62 Joe Mercer.
63 Chris Finnegan.
64 Cradley Heath.
65 Rocky.
66 Ray Reardon.
67 St Louis, USA.
68 Aldershot.
69 Sue Brown.
70 Denis Howell.

2 General 1

 1 The Rugby Football League.
 2 Brian Budd (Canadian Soccer player).
 3 Penny Chuter.
 4 Bob McIntyre.
 5 Phil Read.
 6 Graham Wood.
 7 Kork Ballington of South Africa.
 8 Jock Taylor.
 9 Squaw Valley, in California.
10 Vera Caslavska.
11 The 70-Metre Jump.
12 Willie Davenport (he won the 110-Metres Hurdles in 1968).

Goals

1 Polo.
2 Soccer or handball.
3 Hockey.
4 Lacrosse.
5 Ice hockey.

3 Soccer 1

 1 Bath City.
 2 Worcester City: the score was 2–1.
 3 Bob Stokoe.
 4 Carlos Alberto.
 5 Martin Peters.
 6 Paul Madeley of Leeds.
 7 Ted McDougall of Bournemouth, who scored 42 goals.
 8 Arsenal, in February 1975.
 9 Middlesbrough.
10 George Armstrong: he made 500 appearances between 1960 and 1977.
11 Ron Saunders.
12 Oleg Blokhin: Dynamo Kiev 1975.

4   Boxing 1

1 Don Cockell, in 1951.
2 Dave Charnley.
3 Dai Dower, in 1955.
4 Richard Dunn, who lost to Joe Bugner in 1976.
5 Ingemar Johansson: he was disqualified in the 1952 Olympic final for 'not trying'.
6 Leon and Mike Spinks.
7 Jack Matthews, father of Sir Stanley Matthews.
8 Jack Johnson.
9 The Marquis of Queensbury, who formulated the rules of boxing in the 1750s.
10 Clinton McKenzie (light-welterweight): he lost on points.
11 Ernie Terrell. His sister is Tammie Terrell.
12 Ralph Charles: he was knocked out in round 7.

5   Athletics 1

1 Evelyn Ashford: she won the 100-Metres and 200-Metres.
2 Lasse Viren, as a mark of respect to Brendan Foster.
3 Lancashire.
4 David Bedford (1973).
5 Chris Chataway.
6 In Italy (Florence).
7 The Triple Jump.
8 Hartley (Donna and Bill).
9 Pyoter Bolotnikov of USSR.
10 Steve Jones of Gwent.
11 Derek Ibbotson.
12 Jim Ryun of USA.

Barrier Breakers

Roger Bannister, Derek Ibbotson, Chris Chataway, Ken Wood, Brian Hewsson, Gordon Pirie, Bruce Tulloh.

6 Rugby League 1

1 Steve Hesford of Warrington.
2 Phil Hogan (he actually transferred for £32,000).
3 Dewsbury.
4 Blackpool Borough, in 1954.
5 Broughton Rangers, also known as Belle Vue Rangers.
6 Ian Ball of Barrow and, formerly, Waterloo.
7 Dewsbury (13–2).
8 Brian Lockwood of Widnes.
9 Hunslet, in 1965.
10 Hull, who beat Hull Kingston Rovers in the Final.
11 George Fairburn, who transferred in 1981 from Wigan to Hull Kingston Rovers.
12 Warrington, who beat Barrow 12–5.

7 Soccer 2

1 Allan Brown.
2 Bradford City (by 1–0 in the first leg game).
3 Feyenoord, in 1970.
4 Raddy Avramovic of Notts County.
5 Oxford United, in 1969, followed by Norwich, also in 1969.
6 Hereford, in 1972–3.
7 The World Cup Quarter Final in 1970, in which England lost 3–2 to West Germany.
8 Duncan Forbes of Norwich.
9 Bobby Moncur: he is now at Plymouth.
10 Ray Clarke: he returned to Brighton.
11 Bolton, who were in Division 1 for sixty years.
12 Glossop.

Expensive Transfers

Trevor Francis, Steve Daley, Andy Grey, Kevin Reeves, Clive Allen, Ian Wallace, Kenny Sanson, Garry Birtles, Justin Fashanu, Bryan Robson.

8   Cricket 1

1 Ian Thomson, who took 10 for 49 (Sussex versus Warwickshire, 1964).
2 Mushtaq Mohammed, who had scored 30,777 runs up
 to the beginning of 1981.
3 Derek Underwood.
4 Roy Marshall: 77 minutes, when playing against Bed-
 fordshire in 1968.
5 Swansea.
6 Wilfred Rhodes, 52 years 175 days.
7 John Langridge of Sussex (1928–55).
8 Ken Higgs (Leicester versus Surrey, 1974).
9 Rodney Marsh, with a score of 110 not out.
10 Wilfred Rhodes, in 1899.
11 Lance Gibbs.
12 Mike Brearley.

9   Speedway

1 Rye House.
2 Reading.
3 Jack Milne, in 1937.
4 David Jessup, who was Michael Lee's team mate.
5 Halifax.
6 Reading.
7 Wolverhampton.
8 Kenny Carter.
9 Les Collins of Leicester.
10 Dave Jessup of Kings Lynn.
11 USA: won by Penhall and Shwartz.
12 Reading.

10   General 2

1 Anna Marie Proell of Austria.
2 Oakland Raiders: they beat Philadelphia Eagles 27–10
 in the Final.
3 They all hold Easter Hockey Festivals.

4 Crystal **Palace**.
5 Equestrian and Shooting events.
6 Ski-jumping.
7 Margaret Beck (now Lockwood), in 1973.
8 Gawal Awad of Egypt.
9 Flemming Delfs of Denmark.
10 Karate.
11 Bath.
12 Heather Mackay of Australia.

Baseball

a) Yankees of New York City; b) Pirates of Pittsburgh; c) Cubs of Chicago; d) Athletics of Oakland; e) Phillies of Philadelphia; f) Tigers of Detroit; g) Dodgers of Los Angeles.

11   Athletics 2

1 Mike Boit of Kenya.
2 Valeriy Borzov, in 1972.
3 Dick Fosbury, in 1968.
4 Don Quarrie.
5 Kathy Binns of Yorkshire.
6 Stuart Storey.
7 Dave Bedford, in 1971.
8 At Koblenz, West Germany.
9 Nadyézhda Chizóva of USSR (the Shot title in 1966, 1969, 1971 and 1974).
10 The Stewart family: Ian, Peter and Mary.
11 Kip Keino, in 1966, with a time of 3 minutes 54.4 seconds.
12 Joyce Smith, in 1972.

12   Golf 1

1 Peter Thomson, in 1954 and 1965.
2 Woburn.
3 Bobby Locke of South Africa.
4 Peter Tupling, for a World record 255–29 under par.

  5 Kel Nagle.
  6 Gene Sarazen of USA.
  7 Turnberry.
  8 Bernard Gallagher.
  9 Glen Campbell.
 10 Cypress Point.
 11 Peter Alliss, the television commentator, and his father
    Percy.
 12 Sam Snead.

13   Horse Racing 1

  1 Sagaro, who won in 1975–6–7.
  2 Lord Halifax.
  3 Morston, in 1973.
  4 Bangor on Dee.
  5 Highclere.
  6 Royal Palace, in 1967; the trainer was Noel Murless.
  7 Detroit, in 1980.
  8 In 1973: he was co-favourite with Crisp.
  9 Linda Sheedy.
 10 1947. Mr Black rode Fortina.
 11 Three Troikas, in 1979.
 12 They were Steve Donoghue and Charlie Elliott.

Race-courses

a) Cartmel; b) Liverpool; c) Brighton; d) Taunton; e)
Salisbury; f) Fakenham; g) Wolverhampton; h) Nottingham; i) Chester; j) Perth.

14   Cycling

  1 Hugh Porter.
  2 Mandy Jones of Rochdale.
  3 Graham Jones: he finished in second place, Hinault in
    fourth.
  4 Freddy Maertens.
  5 Lucien Van Impe, in 1976.
  6 Beth Heiden. She won an Olympic Speed Skating Medal

in February 1980, then the World Women's Road Cycling Race in France on August 31.
 7 Bernard Thevenet.
 8 Bill Nickson.
 9 Albert Zweifel.
10 Luxembourg.
11 Tommy Simpson.
12 Eddy Merckx.

15   Soccer 3

 1 Notts County, in 1894.
 2 Michael Robinson: he transferred from Preston North End to Manchester City.
 3 Victorino of Uruguay.
 4 Inter Milan.
 5 Alvin Martin of West Ham.
 6 Manchester United, with 87; followed by Arsenal (77), Liverpool (74) and Spurs (also 74).
 7 Rochdale: 10 defeats up to the end of the 1981–2 competition.
 8 Clydebank.
 9 Netherfield and Bridlington Trinity.
10 Ferenc Puskas.
11 Portsmouth, playing in 1939 versus Wolves.
12 Gylmar.

16   Cricket 2

 1 Archie McLaren, who scored 424 runs in the Lancashire versus Somerset match in 1895.
 2 Ken Barrington, in 1964–5.
 3 Majid Khan of Glamorgan: he scored 200 in 1970.
 4 Middlesex, when playing Yorkshire at Headingley in 1974.
 5 Gary Gilmour.
 6 Wasim Bari of Pakistan, playing against New Zealand in 1978–9.
 7 Lee Irvine, who scored 102 in the match against Australia.

8 Trevor Goddard.
9 Patsy Hendren.
10 John Edrich.
11 Karachi (Pakistan versus West Indies).
12 Doug Slade and Mick Maslin, for Minor Counties: Eastbourne versus Notts, in 1976. This is the only record held by Minor Counties.

County Cricket

Derbyshire, Gloucestershire, Kent, Lancashire, Middlesex, Nottinghamshire, Surrey, Sussex, Yorkshire.

17   Tennis 1

1 Stan Smith and Bob Lutz.
2 India.
3 Neale Fraser, in 1960: he beat Rod Laver.
4 David Lloyd, in 1976.
5 Cliff and Nancy Richey.
6 Hank Pfister and Victor Amaya.
7 Thomas Koch.
8 Billie-Jean King, in 1967.
9 Fred Stolle.
10 Margaret Court.
11 Fred Hoyles.
12 Rosie Casals.

18   Rugby Union 1

1 Willie John McBride, who has made 17 appearances.
2 Tony Ward: he gained 18 points when playing against South Africa in 1980.
3 New Zealand Universities, in 1977, with the result 21–9.
4 The two other players were Alun Lewis and Brynmor Williams.
5 Loughborough Colleges, in 1970 and 1976.
6 Alistair Biggar of London Scottish.
7 Rosslyn Park.

8 Dickie Jeeps.
9 Mike Campbell-Lamerton, in 1966.
10 Ray 'Chico' Hopkins of Maesteg.
11 Peter Enevoldson of Oxford.
12 Neath.

19   Athletics 3

1 The 800-Metres race, when the first three places were won by USSR.
2 The 100-Metres race.
3 Mike Kearns.
4 St Louis, in 1904.
5 Merv Lincoln, in 1958, when he finished second to Elliot.
6 Ian Stewart.
7 The *Three Peaks Race* (Snowdon, Scafell and Ben Nevis).
8 Keith Stock in the Pole Vault: Brian Hooper set a new record at 18 feet 4 inches.
9 Brendan Foster: the 2 miles record of 8 minutes 13.8.0 seconds went to 8 minutes 13.5.0 seconds.
10 Lillian Board, in the 400-Metres.
11 Alberto Salazar of USA.
12 Eammon Coghlan of Ireland.

20   General 3

1 Badminton.
2 Driving with Coach and Horses (team).
3 Sutton Coldfield: they beat Hightown 1–1 and 4–2 on penalties.
4 Tony Meo of Holborn.
5 Curling.
6 Angling: they are names of casting flies.
7 Wind-surfing.
8 Willie Boone.
9 Igor Bobrin of USSR.
10 Yachting: Admirals Cup.

11 Jimmy White of Tooting.
12 Arthur Murray.

Sports Pitches

1 Basketball; 2 Ice hockey; 3 Badminton.

21   Soccer 4

1 David Wagstaff of Blackburn.
2 Nottingham Forest.
3 Hungary: they have won three times.
4 Stockport County, with a score of 3–2 on aggregate.
5 Stirling Albion.
6 Fulham, in games played over two legs.
7 Tony Coton, in the match between Birmingham and Sunderland.
8 Crystal Palace, in 1976.
9 Jock Stein, the Scotland Manager.
10 Hibernian.
11 Tommy Caton of Manchester City.
12 Derek Dooley of Sheffield Wednesday.

We've Won the Cup!

1 F.A. Cup: *first winners*, The Wanderers; *most winners*, Aston Villa who have won it seven times.
2 Football league Cup: *first winners*, Aston Villa; *most winners* Aston Villa who have won it three times.
3 European Cup: *first winners*, Real Madrid; *most winners*, Real Madrid who have won it six times.
4 Jules Rimet Trophy (the World Cup); *first winner*, Uruguary; *most winners*, Brazil, who have won it three times. (After their third win, the trophy in the illustration was given to Brazil to keep permanently, and the Cup now in competition is a different design, called the FIFA World Cup.)
5 FA Challenge Trophy: *first winners*, Macclesfield Town; *most winners*, Scarborough, who have won it three times.
6 Scottish FA Cup; *first winners*, Queens Park; *most winners*, Celtic, who have won it twenty-six times.

22   Boxing 2

1 Wilfredo Gomez (Light-featherweight) and Ayub Kalule (Light-middleweight).
2 They were both knocked out after 2 minutes 27 seconds of Round 4.
3 José Legra.
4 Laslo Papp of Hungary (Light-middleweight and Middleweight): 1948–56.
5 Paul Pender.
6 Roy Gumbs of Tottenham.
7 Walter McGowan (Flyweight): stopped on cuts in Round 7.
8 Joey Singleton (1974–5).
9 Ruben Olivares (Californian Mexican).
10 Tommy Burns of Canada, in 1910.
11 Steve Early.
12 James J. Braddock (knocked out in Round 8): 1937.

23   Tennis 2

1 Gene Mayer: in one of the Group Matches.
2 Fred Perry. (The first player to win all four in the same year was Donald Budge.)
3 Roger Taylor.
4 The winners of the Men's Doubles at Wimbledon.
5 Ann Hobbs, who beat Kathy Jordan.
6 Paul McNamee and Peter McNamara of Australia.
7 Stan Smith in 1972: he beat Ilie Nastase.
8 Françoise Durr.
9 Angela Buxton in 1956, playing against Shirley Fry.
10 Maureen Connolly, in 1953.
11 Victor Amaya.
12 Ilie Nastase.

24   Rugby Union 2

1 Leicester, when England beat Ireland 23–5.
2 Mike Burton, whilst playing against Australia, in 1975.
3 Peter Butler.

4 John Pullin.
5 It was made in India out of the rupees left in the bank by
  the disbanded Calcutta Rugby Club in 1878.
6 At the Oval cricket ground, when playing against Scotland.
7 Ion Constantin of Romania.
8 Graeme Higginson.
9 Hugo Porta of Argentina.
10 The Gazelles.
11 Alan Hewson.
12 Mark Loane of Australia.

25   Snooker and Darts

1 Fred Davis.
2 John Spencer.
3 Eddie Charlton of Australia, in 1972.
4 Patsy Fagan, in 1977.
5 Perrie Mans.
6 Alex Higgins.
7 Bill Lennard.
8 Stefan Lord of Sweden, who has won it twice.
9 Bobby George.
10 167.
11 Tony Brown.
12 Cliff Lazarenko, who finished behind Eric Bristow and
   John Lowe.

26   Horse Racing 2

1 Right Tack, in 1969: in the 2000-Guineas.
2 Waterloo.
3 La Lagune, in 1968.
4 Alec Russell.
5 Two miles.
6 John Burke, in 1976.
7 Ayr.
8 Citation, in 1948.
9 Hamilton Park.

10 Ascot, in the 1966–7 season.
11 R. Houghton, in 1967 and 1968.
12 John Gorton.

Grand National

Valentines: 9 & 25; Bechers Brook: 6 & 22; Water Jump: 16; Canal Turn: 8 & 24; The Chair: 15.

27   Golf 2

1 Cherry Hills in USA.
2 The US Masters Course at Augusta.
3 At St Andrews: they make up the four courses along with the New and Old courses.
4 Bernard Gallacher, who finished third. (He lost to Greg Norman.)
5 Sam Torrance with 282 – Ballesteros 284.
6 Royal Birkdale.
7 Canada.
8 Mark James, who was joint third.
9 A belt: 1860–1870.
10 Mark Hayes of USA.
11 Muirfield, in Ohio.
12 Bobby Jones, in 1930.

28   Athletics 4

1 Janis Lusis of USSR: he won the Javelin title in 1962, 1966, 1969 and 1971.
2 David Wottle.
3 Joyce Smith, in just under two and a half hours.
4 The High Jump, in 1948 and 1956.
5 Andrea Lynch, in the 100-Metres Race.
6 Mel Batty of Southend.
7 John Landy of Australia, with a time of 3 minutes 58.0 seconds.
8 Twice, the first time at Oxford; the second at Vancouver – in the Commonwealth Games.
9 Harald Schmid of West Germany, in 1977.

10 Lee Calhoun, in 1956 and 1960.
11 José Joao da Silva of Brazil.
12 Gaston Roelants of Belgium: 3000-Metres Steeple-
    chase Gold Medallist in 1964.

29   Boxing 3

1 St Helens: the Gilbody brothers, and Keith Wallace.
2 Lotte Mwale.
3 Tony Sibson.
4 Alexis Arguello, who beat Jim Watt in 1981.
5 Pat Cowdell (Featherweight).
6 Danny McAlinden of Northern Ireland.
7 Dai Dower (Flyweight), in 1957.
8 Jim (his real name was George, but he boxed as Jim).
9 Henry Armstrong.
10 Max Baer.
11 Len Hutchins in 1977 at Liverpool; the fight was stop-
    ped in Round 3.
12 George Chuvalo.

Heavyweight Champions

1 a) Joe Louis; b) he beat James J. Braddock first; c)
Tommy Farr took him to fifteen rounds.

2 a) Muhammed Ali; b) his nickname was The Louisville
Lip, c) he fought one World Heavyweight title fight under
his former name, Cassius Clay.

30   Cricket 3

1 B. P. Bracewell of New Zealand.
2 Roy Booth of Worcestershire, in 1964.
3 Conrad Hunte.
4 Mike Hendrick.
5 Middlesex.
6 Gordon Greenidge, who made 177 for Hampshire versus Glamorgan in 1975.
7 Brian Rose.
8 Bill Athey of Yorkshire.

9 Raman Subba Row, the Tour Manager of the 1981–2
  Tour to India.
10 Asif Iqbal, in the Kent versus Lancashire match of 1971.
11 Roy Swetman.
12 Somerset.

31   General 4

1 Liechtenstein.
2 Basketball.
3 Bulgaria.
4 Real Tennis.
5 Cycling.
6 Lasham, near Alton, in Hampshire.
7 Snooker.
8 Fencing.
9 Chris Brasher.
10 Alex 'Hurricane' Higgins.
11 Bobsleighing (in the World Championships).
12 Basketball: he plays for Crystal Palace.

32   Soccer 5

1 Ivan Buljan of Yugoslavia.
2 Alan Rough.
3 Brian Clough.
4 Oldham Athletic.
5 David Jack.
6 Zico of Brazil.
7 In Rome: the 1977 Final.
8 Carlo Sartori: he went to Bologna.
9 Kim Book, the brother of Tony Book.
10 Johnny Aston.
11 Aston Villa.
12 1974.

Cup Finals

Kennington Oval, Lillie Bridge, Fallowfield, Goodison
Park, Crystal Palace, Old Trafford, Stamford Bridge,
Wembley.

33   Show Jumping

1 Hickstead.
2 Anne Moore, in 1972, on the horse Psalm.
3 Michael Mac.
4 George Bowman (Coach and Fours).
5 Michael Whittaker, who beat his brother John Whittaker into second place.
6 Captain Mark Phillips: he and Lucinda Prior Palmer each won four times.
7 Hugo Simon of Austria.
8 Moxy.
9 1960.
10 Manhattan.
11 John Whittaker.
12 Graham Fletcher.

34   Motor Racing 1

1 Ritchie Ginther.
2 John Surtees, who switched from Ferrari to Cooper Maserati.
3 Vanwall.
4 Pat Moss, Stirling's sister.
5 Derek Bell.
6 He won by 4½ minutes.
7 A foot and mouth epidemic.
8 Timo Makkinen.
9 Bobby Unser.
10 The 1977 Japanese Grand Prix.
11 The late Mike Hailwood.
12 Goodwood. He retired until 1980.

Grand Prix Circuits

1 *Belgium*, Zolder; 2 *Holland*, Zandvoort; 3 *Spain*, Jarama; 4 *South Africa*, Kyalami; 5 *West Germany*, Hockenheim.

35   Rugby Union 3

1 London Scottish, who beat Wasps 7–3 in the Final.
2 London Welsh.
3 Naas Botha of South Africa, in the match against Ireland in 1981. (Ireland lost 12–10, but scored the only try.)
4 Peter Kirsten – according to the press, the best fly-half against whom the 1974 Tourists had played.
5 Bob Hiller.
6 Garryowen.
7 Wynand Claasen, who took over from Mornie du Plessis.
8 Noel Murphy.
9 Gala.
10 Northumberland, who beat Gloucestershire 15–6 in the Final.
11 He beat Phil Bennett's record.
12 There were no Anglos in the team (i.e. players with English clubs).

36   Cricket 4

1 Kapil Dev of India.
2 Alan Davidson.
3 Bobby Simpson, with 359 runs in a State Match, and 311 when playing versus England in 1963–4–5.
4 Gary Cosier, who scored 109 in 1975–6, when playing versus West Indies.
5 Nick Pocock of Hampshire.
6 Grace Road, Leicester.
7 John Steele of Leicestershire, and David Steele of Derbyshire.
8 The son of Terry Downes.
9 A. C. Smith (Assistant Manager), playing against Jamaica.
10 Glamorgan.
11 Gloucestershire.
12 Clive Lloyd, in 1980.

37   Swimming

1 Philip Hubble.
2 Tracey Caulkins.
3 Charles Hickock.
4 Felipe Munoz of Mexico.
5 Mike Wenden of Australia.
6 Debbie Meyer of USA.
7 Brian Brinkley.
8 Hungary.
9 Don Schollander, in 1964.
10 At Utrecht, for the 100-Metres Freestyle event in the 1966 European Championships.
11 Judy Grinham, for the Backstroke event in 1956.
12 Klaudia Kolb of USA.

38   Soccer 6

1 Alan Gowling.
2 Frankie Gray: he played for Leeds in 1975, and for Nottingham Forest in 1980.
3 Loughborough Town.
4 Bruce Bannister and Alan Warboys: they were prolific scorers at that time, when playing with Bristol Rovers.
5 Wolverhampton Wanderers.
6 FC Cologne.
7 West Ham.
8 Barrow.
9 Middlesbrough: they won 6–1 against Norwich City.
10 George Raynor of Southampton.
11 Glasgow Celtic.
12 Klaus Allofs, in the match between West Germany and Holland.

World Cup, World Cup

Ron Springett, Jimmy Armfield, Ray Wilson, Ron Flowers, John Connelly, George Eastham, Jimmy Greaves, Roger Hunt, Bobby Charlton.

39   Tennis 3

1 The Italian Championships: the *Foro Italico* is a part of Rome's Olympic complex.
2 John Newcombe, in 1971.
3 Ken Rosewall.
4 Sandy Mayer.
5 William Renshaw: 1881–6.
6 Ivan Lendl.
7 Mike Sangster from Torquay, with 65 appearances.
8 Angela Mortimer also from Torquay, in 1961.
9 John Feaver.
10 The Japanese Open: her first win for seven years.
11 Brian Gottfried, who lost to Borg.
12 Brian Teacher of USA.

40   Horse Racing 3

1 Aureole, who finished second in Pinza's Derby of 1953.
2 Victor Morley-Lawson.
3 Tommy Weston.
4 Mill Reef, in 1971.
5 The Hennessy Gold Cup.
6 Beldale Flutter, in 1980.
7 Meld, in 1955: this filly won the 1000-Guineas, the Oaks and the St Leger.
8 Admetus.
9 Guy Harwood.
10 Jenny Pitman: this was the first Treble for a woman trainer.
11 G. Smyth.
12 Peter Nelson.

41   Athletics 5

1 David Jenkins.
2 Ross Hepburn, High Jump 1977, age 15 years 10 months.
3 Paula Fudge of Great Britain.
4 Collette Besson.

5 Alan Pascoe.
6 Bob Beamon: 29 feet 2¼ inches.
7 Brendan Foster, who won a Bronze Medal in the 10,000-Metres.
8 Chris Brasher.
9 Steve Ovett.
10 Brian Hooper.
11 Steve Cram.
12 Mark Holtom, who won a Gold Medal in the 110-Metres Hurdles.

Fill in the Blanks

1956 Men's 800-Metres, Derek Johnson; *1964 Marathon*, Basil Heatley.

1960 Men's 100-Metres, Peter Radford; *1972 Men's 1500-Metres*, Ian Stewart; *1968 Men's 400-Metres Hurdles, first* David Hemery, *third* John Sherwood; 1952 3000-Metres Steeplechase, John Disley.

42   Golf 3

1 Tom Watson.
2 Hal Sutton of USA, with a score of 276.
3 Bob Charles of New Zealand.
4 Greg Norman.
5 Tom Kite of USA.
6 Sandy Lyle.
7 Lindrick.
8 Sandy Lyle, in 1980.
9 Kent.
10 Lee Trevino, in 1971 and 1972.
11 Neil Coles.
12 Mark James.

43   Boxing 4

1 Wilfred Benitez, when he beat Maurice Hope.
2 Colin Jones (Welterweight).

3 Bunny Sterling.
4 John Henry Lewis (the Light-heavyweight Champion).
5 Joe Louis, former World Heavyweight Champion.
6 Johnny and Ray Famechon.
7 Ken Buchanan, in 1973.
8 Gene Fullmer.
9 Nel Tarleton.
10 Jerry Quarry.
11 Tommy Farr.
12 Brian London.

44   Rugby Union 4

1 Bruce Robertson.
2 Mike Gibson.
3 Ian Kirkpatrick.
4 The letter 'O'.
5 Llanelli.
6 Leicester.
7 The Barbarians.
8 Stuart Lane of Cardiff. He twisted knee ligaments as he turned to tackle an opponent just after the kick-off in the first match.
9 St Luke's College Exeter – now amalgamated with Exeter University.
10 Guys.
11 Both Ian Peck of Cambridge University and Nick Mallet of Oxford University missed the Varsity Match.
12 Newport.

Rugby Union Caps

Mike Gibson (69); J. P. R. Williams (55); Roland Betranne (50); Willie John McBride (63); Tom Kiernan (54); Benoit Dauga (50); Colin E. Meads (55); Gareth Edwards (53); Sandy Carmichael (50).

45   General 5

1 Croquet.
2 Six.
3 They have a tip-off.
4 Motor Racing.
5 Scott Hamilton of USA.
6 300.
7 The World Table Tennis Championships.
8 *Gretel II*.
9 Denise Beilmann of Switzerland.
10 Debbie Cottrill.
11 USA.
12 Bolton Wanderers.

46   Soccer 7

1 Arsenal. They were in sixth place in 1915, and were promoted in 1919 after World War I.
2 £600.
3 Newport County.
4 Fred Keenor.
5 Alberto Tarantini, who played for Birmingham.
6 Jimmy and Brian Greenhoff, in 1977, playing for Manchester United.
7 Hurucan.
8 Willie Ormond.
9 Czechoslovakia.
10 Carlisle United.
11 Norwich City 1981–2.
12 Harlow Town. The score was 1–1, with a replay: 1–0.

Football League Clubs

a) Swansea City; b) Blackpool; c) York City; d) Newcastle United; e) Norwich City; f) Colchester United; g) Brighton & Hove Albion; h) Bournemouth; i) Exeter City; j) Lincoln City.

47   Cricket 5

1 Cross Arrows.
2 Ken Barrington.
3 Peter May.
4 Len Pascoe.
5 Derbyshire.
6 Derek Shackleton.
7 Barry Wood, with 10 Gold Awards (he played then for Lancashire, but now plays for Derbyshire).
8 Brisbane, in 1960–1: Australia versus West Indies.
9 Jackie Hampshire.
10 Mike Gatting, in the Middlesex versus MCC match.
11 Richard Hayward: Hampshire versus Sri Lanka.
12 Mushtaq Mohammed: 100 not out at Trent Bridge.

48   Horse Racing 4

1 Henry Cecil: the amount was £684,000.
2 The November Handicap.
3 Bob Davies, who has ridden approximately nine hundred winners.
4 Willie Shoemaker.
5 Newbury.
6 Glint of Gold.
7 Gay Spartan.
8 Moorestyle: the first sprinter for fifteen years.
9 Gordon Richards.
10 Noel Murless: he trained Crepello and Carrozza, winners in 1957.
11 The Dikler in 1973.
12 Usually an apprentice. Major jockeys have their names printed on boards before a race, but little-known ones are only 'chalked up'.

49   Motor Racing 2

1 Jacques Lafitte.
2 Brian Henton.

3 The South African.
4 Brabham.
5 Carlos Reutemann, in 1978.
6 Derek Daly.
7 Alain Prost, who won the French Grand Prix.
8 Italy had seven, to France's six (although the French
   had a greater number of winners!).
9 Patrick Tambay.
10 Nelson Piquet.
11 Nigel Mansell.
12 Giancarlo Baghetti of Italy, who won the 1961 French
   Grand Prix at Rheims.

Where Are They?

1 Watkins Glen; 2 Monaco; 3 Brands Hatch.

50   Rugby League 2

1 Huddersfield.
2 Ray Ashby and Brian Gabbittas.
3 The two players were Mal Aspey and Dave Eckersley,
   both from Widnes.
4 Keighley.
5 Leeds, in 1941–2 and 1977–8.
6 Warrington, in 1974, 1978 and 1981.
7 Oldham.
8 Halifax, when they beat Wakefield 22–11.
9 Sammy Lloyd, in the Hull versus Leeds match, also
   played in 1980.
10 Rochdale Hornets, 24–8 January 1981.
11 Gerry Helme of Warrington, in 1950 and 1954.
12 Jim Sullivan of Wigan.

51   Tennis 4

1 Bobby Riggs, in 1939; he did not defend the titles after
   World War II.
2 Roscoe Tanner.

3 Yannick Noah (by Eric Fromm), although Lendl and
  Pecci were also defeated on the same afternoon.
4 He won the 'Junior' Grand Slam – the Under-eighteen
  events of the 'Big Four'.
5 Henri Cochet's record.
6 In the 1980 Masters Final, whilst playing against Mc-
  Enroe.
7 Ann Jones, with Christine Janes third.
8 18–16.
9 Rafael Osuna of Mexico and Denis Ralston of USA
  (7–5; 6–3; 10–8).
10 David Lloyd.
11 Mats Wilander of Sweden.
12 Arthur Ashe, in 1976.

52   Cricket 6

1 Peter Willey, in 1981.
2 Mike 'Pasty' Harris (now Notts: 1971).
3 Bishen Bedi: 1961–80.
4 Graham Dilley.
5 Tony Greig.
6 Alan Knott.
7 Aftab Baloch: aged 16 years 191 days when he played
  versus New Zealand, 1969–70.
8 Queensland, who beat Western Australia in the Final.
9 Brian Sellers: 1933–46.
10 Northants, who lost to Oxford in 1973, and to Combined Universities in 1975.
11 Fenner Trophy.
12 W. Hogg of Warwickshire, N. G. B. Cook of Leicestershire, and D. M. Smith of Surrey.

Cricket Champions

County Championship: 1975 Leicestershire, 1977 Mid-
dlesex and Kent; John Player: 1973 Kent, 1979 Somerset;
Gillette Cup: 1971 Lancashire, 1978 Sussex; Benson &
Hedges: 1974 Surrey, 1977 Gloucestershire.

53   General 6

1 Argentina – the Championship was last contested in 1936.
2 Innsbruck, Austria, in 1964.
3 Chris Baillieu.
4 Hugh Porter, World Cycling Pursuit Champion in 1972 and 1973.
5 The Boat Race.
6 Purple.
7 Mohbullah Khan.
8 Biathlon.
9 Ian Day of Doncaster.
10 Wimbledon.
11 Denis Neale: Table Tennis International.
12 Basketball.

54   Horse Racing 5

1 Boldboy.
2 Newton Abbot.
3 John Matthias.
4 Frank Buckle (Lester Piggott's score is 25).
5 Arkle.
6 Edward Hide.
7 Spartan Missile.
8 They were Giafranco Dettori, who won the 2000-Guineas; and Johnny Roe, winner of the 1000-Guineas.
9 Neville Selwood, in 1962.
10 Reg Hollinshead.
11 Terry Biddlecombe, in 1965 and 1966.
12 The Dewhurst Stakes.

55   Soccer 8

1 Wimbledon: sixteen players were sent off in the team's first two hundred matches.
2 Sunderland.
3 Kilmarnock, when competing for the Anglo-Scots Cup.
4 Bristol Rovers, on Lee's debut for Spurs.

5 Plymouth Argyle.
6 David and Pierce O'Leary of Eire.
7 Billy Bremner, in 1970.
8 Southampton: they lost to Watford in the second leg of the League Cup.
9 Kevin Reeves of Manchester City.
10 Peter Taylor of Crystal Palace.
11 Nottingham Forest: 1977–8.
12 Matt Busby.

Travellin' Light

1 Derek Dougan: Aston Villa; 2 Trevor Hockey; Sheffield United; 3 Hugh McIlmoyle: Carlisle United; 4 Tony Hateley: Chelsea.

56   Cricket 7

1 Laurie Potter of Kent.
2 Gary Palmer of Somerset for school holidays. (He is the son of the umpire, Ken Palmer.)
3 Sarfraz Nawaz (Pakistan versus West Indies).
4 Lancashire.
5 The Cowdreys: Colin in 1973 and Chris in 1978.
6 Ali Bacher.
7 John Dyson.
8 Geoff Boycott.
9 Colin Cowdrey, with a total of 38 half-centuries.
10 Bristol City.
11 Clive Lloyd, who overtook P. B. H. May's record of 41 Tests in 1980.
12 By 2 points: 304 to 302.

57   Golf 4

1 Gordon Brand.
2 US Masters.
3 Prestwick.
4 Argentina, in 1953.
5 William Whitelaw, the Home Secretary.

   6 Muriel Thomson.
   7 Bruce Crampton of Australia (the year before Gary
     Player).
   8 Scotland.
   9 Baldovina Dassu of Italy.
  10 David Graham, in 1976.
  11 Sam Snead, in 1960–1–2.
  12 Michelle Walker, who beat Karsten Erland of Sweden
     in the Final.

58   General 7

   1 Five.
   2 Eugene Hughes of Ireland.
   3 Motocross.
   4 Desmond Douglas.
   5 Lacca Champion.
   6 Jim Rempe of USA.
   7 Gyorgy Bardos of Hungary.
   8 Four.
   9 Queens Park Rangers.
  10 Bowls: awarded for the Team All Round title in the
     World Bowls Championship.
  11 Baron Pierre de Coubertain, in 1896.
  12 Eric Heiden, for Speed Skating: he won five Gold
     Medals.

Which Game?

1 Soccer or water polo; 2 Polo; 3 Hockey; 4 Cricket;
5 Lawn Tennis; 6 Table Tennis.

59   Horse Racing 6

   1 The Great Britain versus USA Jockeys' Cham-
     pionships: in USA.
   2 Doncaster.
   3 Sir Ivor, in 1968.
   4 Ayr.
   5 L'Escargot.

6 Fulke Walwyn, in 1962.
7 Fred Winter, in 1965 and 1966.
8 Chester, near the banks of the Dee.
9 Lester Piggott.
10 Dunfermline, the Queen's Horse, who won in 1977.
11 Christy Roche: he had 68 wins.
12 Alleged, in 1977 and 1978.

60   Cricket 8

1 John Edrich, Captain in 1974–5, in the Test versus Australia.
2 Kent, in 1976, 1977 and 1978.
3 Somerset.
4 Wayne Daniel. (The 7–12 is still a competition 'best'.)
5 Sunil Gavaskar of Somerset, after two Benson and Hedges innings of 90 and 123.
6 Sir Jack Hobbs, with 197: he scored his 100th in 1923.
7 Fred Titmus.
8 Trevor Bailey, in 1959.
9 Mike Gatting (Middlesex) and Steve Gatting (Brighton).
10 Basil Williams of the West Indies.
11 Mike Denness: Kent in 1976, and Essex in 1979.
12 Asif Iqbal of Kent.

61   Soccer 9

1 Leeds United, who gained 64 points in 1970–1: Arsenal won the title, with 65 points.
2 Jimmy Nicholl of Manchester United.
3 Newcastle United.
4 Ipswich Town, in 1978.
5 Bobby Charlton.
6 *L'Equipe*.
7 Bradford Park Avenue.
8 Clive Allen.
9 Southend United.

10 Dynamo Zagreb: the 1967 Fairs Cup.
11 Juste Fontaine of France, in 1958.
12 Middlesbrough.